IN YOUR MOMENT

Mastering Your Leadership Thresholds

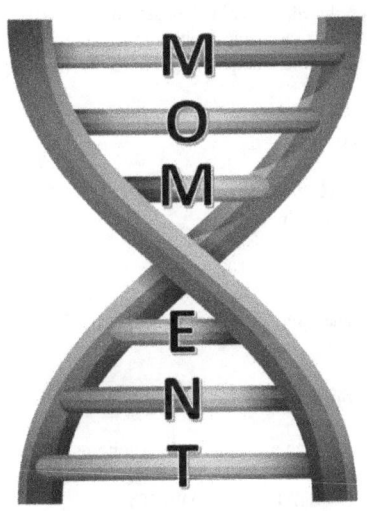

DR. DOUGLAS LINDSAY & DR. JOSEPH BALSKUS

outskirts
press

In Your Moment
Mastering Your Leadership Thresholds
All Rights Reserved.
Copyright © 2024 Dr. Douglas Lindsay & Dr. Joseph Balskus
v2.0

The opinions expressed in this manuscript are solely the opinions of the author and do not represent the opinions or thoughts of the publisher. The author has represented and warranted full ownership and/or legal right to publish all the materials in this book.

This book may not be reproduced, transmitted, or stored in whole or in part by any means, including graphic, electronic, or mechanical without the express written consent of the publisher except in the case of brief quotations embodied in critical articles and reviews.

Outskirts Press, Inc.
http://www.outskirtspress.com

Paperback ISBN: 978-1-9772-7075-7
Hardback ISBN: 978-1-9772-7076-4

Library of Congress Control Number: 2023924176

Cover Photo © 2024 Douglas Lindsay & Joseph Balskus. All rights reserved - used with permission.

Cover Design by Eric M. Sloan & Cole Lindsay

Outskirts Press and the "OP" logo are trademarks belonging to Outskirts Press, Inc.

PRINTED IN THE UNITED STATES OF AMERICA

Table of Contents

Foreword i
Chapter 1: Why This Book? 1
Chapter 2: The Story of Bruno 11
Chapter 3: Foundational Framework for Moments:
Who Do I Say I Am? 21
Chapter 4: "Types" of Moments 33
Chapter 5: M – Minute Points in Time That Present 51
Chapter 6: What Are My Points in Time? 61
Chapter 7: O – Opportunities That 73
Chapter 8: What Are My Opportunities? 83
Chapter 9: M – Manifest into Actions 95
Chapter 10: What Are My Actions? 103
Chapter 11: E – Empowering Us to 115
Chapter 12: What Does Empowering Mean to Me? . 125
Chapter 13: N – Navigate Choices Which Determine Our... 137
Chapter 14: What Do I Need to Navigate? 149
Chapter 15: T – Threshold for Decisions and Ensuing Consequences 159

Chapter 16:   What Thresholds Do I Have? 169

Chapter 17: How Can I Be Sure? The Power of
                    Accountability 183

Chapter 18: What This Means for You 195

Chapter 19: Your Turn 201

About the Authors 207

Foreword

IN LIFE, THERE are moments where a situation or opportunity demands your presence and readiness. Your actions in these moments will draw from your lived experiences, mental readiness, education, and other abilities, all of which impact the outcome, positively or negatively. Have you ever wondered why someone always seems to be in the right place at the right time? Why were they promoted and not you? What sets them apart in life? These were questions I asked myself often until I realized the answer lay within me. Whether out of fear of failure, perfectionism, arrogance, or for other reasons, we often fail to show up, ready for the moment. Can you recall a time when "the moment" presented itself? Were you ready? Did you seize it?

In this book, Dr. Lindsay and Dr. Balskus present the reader with TEMPUS, a framework illustrating the discernible aspects of such moments. They share intentional ways to engage with these aspects, maximizing opportunities while preparing for subsequent moments. With decades of experience as leaders, educators, and professional coaches, the authors bring unquestionable credibility to the TEMPUS model.

While reading the book, I found that moment in my life that shaped me. It was during my time as an enlisted Army soldier when I found myself stuck and unfulfilled, grappling with boredom and uncertainty. I knew I needed to prepare myself to advance my career and improve my lot in life. I aspired to become a military officer, and to achieve that, I needed to take action, make sacrifices, and prioritize it above all other wants. I needed to transform negative energy into positive energy. This necessitated attending college in a nontraditional way, at nights and weekends, eventually earning my degree. This committed action shaped my future, allowing me to be prepared when pivotal moments arrived. I took control, maximized the opportunity, and eventually became an officer. While it may sound simple, I often ponder how different my life would be without that decision.

In this example, education was crucial, but in other moments, you may need a broader set of experiences or competencies, requiring you to do the hard work—to do what others are unwilling to do. Or maybe it is choosing to become a better person, working on being kind to others and to stop being a jerk. Remember, you don't have to be the most intelligent person in the room; instead, you should work on being the most prepared with unwavering determination. I believe it is essential to strive for excellence and refuse to settle for the status quo—and this too requires work in your moments. Finally, teamwork is vital; bringing others alongside you with complementary competencies is critical and is what makes you smarter than others in the room.

Staying prepared for the moment has positioned me to attain greater leadership roles year over year by maintaining this restless, reflective, and perpetual learning mindset. This active approach certainly helped in securing my current role as a CEO. I vowed never to allow myself to be caught off guard or unprepared for when the eventual next moment arrives—and it certainly will.

In conclusion, wishing, resenting, or desiring something different or better won't suffice. You must actively show up and be ready when the moment arrives. I encourage you to use Lindsay and Balskus' TEMPUS framework to further develop yourself as a leader, parent, or neighbor. Remember, life is fleeting, so seize the moment by preparing in the present. Put in the daily work to be better. Your great moment is just around the corner! Will you be ready when the moment shows up?

Dr. Anthony Hassan
President & CEO
Cohen Veterans Network

Chapter 1
WHY THIS BOOK?

"Do what you can, with what you have, where you are."
— Theodore Roosevelt

THE REVEREND BILLY GRAHAM stepped up to the podium after receiving the Congressional Gold Medal for a life of service and accomplishments. At a particular point in his mesmerizing comments, he told the crowd that on numerous occasions he had walked in Statuary Hall, finely adorned with marble carvings of America's leaders, and had gazed at the historic figures. Piercing the audience with his intense eyes, he said these great American figures had one thing in common: "They were all dead." The one common reality of all human life, Graham poignantly stated, is that "we are all going to die." This powerful statement brought everyone in that room face to face with their inevitable reality and prompts anyone to reflect on this inexorable truth.

Hearing that life is finite springs to the forefront of our thoughts the contemplation of questions such as, "How much time do I have remaining?" and "How am I spending the time that I have?" The blunt reality is that we may not like the notion of this mortality, but we cannot dispute it. Since we do not have the certainty of knowing how long that time will actually be, we are left with the present time in which to have influence and impact.

We live in a reality that exists within a temporal framework. While we don't have the certainty of knowing how much of that time we have left, we do have the present. The moments in time that we live each day define us and set us in motion for the next day and the next. With this truism in mind, it causes one to think of the impact we are making with the life and time we have been given. You may have asked yourself before, "What is my impact?" or "What have I done today that has significance?" These are weighty questions and are based on a number of factors, beliefs, and priorities we have imposed upon our lives. Common to all of us, however, is that we must make amends with the time we do have and the moments we live. That is exactly what this book is positioned to help you do. To answer the question, "How can you maximize the moments you do have to ensure that you show up to and excel in them?" To support this question, we have devised a way for us to assess and perform in the moments we encounter.

Generally, when picking up a book to evaluate, two questions will invariably come to mind. The first is, who is writing the book? This is the credibility check. The second has to do with what the book is about and you ask, how will it speak to me? This is the interest check. Both checks are important as they provide the foundation for the subsequent question of, "Do I want to spend what limited time I have available for my personal development on this book?" Let's briefly address these two items upfront.

The first question is the "who" one. This is a book addressing development, primarily your development as a leader. Much like any domain, there are many perspectives on the topic of leadership, and thousands of books are written about it each year. In fact, almost 50 years ago, Ralph Stogdill said, "... there are almost as many different definitions of leadership as there are persons who have attempted to define the concept." He said that in 1974. Fast-forward to today, and how many different perspectives do you think we now have on leadership?

In your own development, you have likely read about several of those perspectives. As you can imagine, however, the rigor

WHY THIS BOOK?

that went into many of those conceptualizations of leadership varies greatly. We set out with a commitment to be careful consumers of the information that is out there, as not all of it is vetted in the same way. This is especially true if we are thinking about a subject that not only affects us but those around us. While many may profess to be experts in leadership, we would posit no one should afford themselves such a title. Effective leadership and leader development is a mountain without a top. It is a process of becoming that lasts a lifetime. It is not an endpoint, but a journey.

It is this journey that brought us to the specific information we are excited to share. Because of our immutable pursuit of leader development, we present a leadership approach that is uniquely penetrating and applicable to anyone's growth journey. Our perspective is based on decades of experience, engagement, and learning. It is fueled by thousands of hours of study and countless conversations with leaders at all levels. This work is a summation of two careers which combine experience from different domains of the workforce. On the applied side, fifty-plus years of those were in military service. This involved leading at the lowest levels up to, and including, the general officer (senior executive) level. That experience involved peacetime as well as deployed environments. It included operational, training, educational, and command assignments. It involved experiences as professors at multiple universities of higher education like the United States Air Force Academy, The Citadel, and The Pennsylvania State University. It also included establishing and running consulting companies where we advised and worked within numerous Fortune 500 companies as well as government agencies.

From a foundational (education) standpoint, we hold multiple advanced degrees in leadership and psychology. We have read and studied thousands of research articles and hundreds of books related to leadership and development. We have hundreds of publications and presentations related to leadership, development, and character. We have set up leadership programs and run leadership programs around the world.

Additionally, in our various roles, we have mentored hundreds of people as leaders and also worked with hundreds of leaders in our roles as executive coaches. To round out this experience, we have also interviewed numerous leaders in different domains such as educational leaders, professional athletes, nonprofit presidents, senior military professionals, entrepreneurs, and heads of organizations. This was done to glean insights from their experiences across different contexts and organizations so we could distill that experience into tangible learning outcomes.

So, the "who" question is a summation of our background, and this is coupled with our passion for developing ourselves and others and sharing our life experiences, both personal and professional. We feel that we, as all should, will never be off our developmental journey as leaders. However, for us, for now, what we discovered was compelling, and we felt it was of the utmost importance to pause, document, capture, and share a unique and special perspective that we believe will help you on your own journey not just as leaders, but as individuals. We joyfully want to share a perspective that our odyssey through leader development (our own and others') has revealed to us, IN THIS MOMENT.

As for the "what" question, we offer a distillation of learning

WHY THIS BOOK?

on the topic of leadership and how we can utilize that to show up for, and succeed in, the moments we encounter in our lives. We offer this book as an opportunity to develop. To learn. To grow. To lead. To succeed.

Turning the pages of this book, you will be embarking on a personal journey with us. Take notes as we strategically and methodically break down our model, which encompasses the very temporal framework of a moment. It begins with a minute point in time when you first encounter your moment and ends when you come face to face with what we have defined as your thresholds. In between the two are four other components that offer a glimpse into yourself as a person, a spouse, a father, a mother, an employee, a leader, and how you perform in the moments you face. The model we offer began with our fascination and subsequent research around the countless occurrences experienced by ourselves and others who made decisions inside a finite point in time. Decisions that resulted in small to monumental trajectory changes in life. From this emerged our *Tempus Model*, which is a practical and meaningful model for human behavior that occurs within a moment and offers an increased awareness of the impactful nature of each step you take before accepting the consequences of your decision.

As we unfold and dissect the *Tempus Model*, you will be compelled to evaluate this notion of time within a moment. Your moment. To supplement your appetite for understanding you and your moments, we will present examples of those who made tremendous decisions that had favorable consequences and those who failed to maximize the moments they had by choices they made (or didn't make). We will wind through the entire decision process within the moment and also evaluate why some people successfully navigate moments, while others seem to have moments and consequences they regret. Moreover, we will emphasize how precious and special our moments are by initially offering an example of someone who experienced an unexpected moment. A moment no one ever wants to face but may encounter. Someone who had a promising life cut short yet, while they lived, capitalized on purposefully and effectively living each and every moment they had remaining. So here is the question before you today:

> How will you choose to live your time, and the moments that make up your time?

Notice we said "live YOUR time," because it is that time that makes up your life. How you choose to invest into that time will result in the quality of your life lived. These are your moments. Since you don't directly control the amount of time you have, you are left to have significance in the moments that you do have and currently live in. Therefore, as you embark on this journey, ask yourself questions such as:

- How are you showing up to your moments?
- How are you maximizing your moments?
- How is your life impacted by the decisions in your moments?
- How can you prepare for your next moments?

For those interested in development, these are the types of questions you will wrestle with. The point of this book is to

WHY THIS BOOK?

help you examine your moments, prepare for these moments, and enact behaviors that are consistent with how you want to be as a person and as a leader in those moments. In addition, inside of the *Tempus Model*, we want you to examine what thresholds have been established in your life so that when you come face to face with them, you will know whether to turn back, level off, retreat, or perhaps move through what might be a perceived threshold that is actually holding you back.

This reading, this learning, must be personal. Your moments will be different from ours. Your preparation, and ultimately your reaction, is not able to be determined by us because only you personally face each day. However, our research and model will offer an increased level of consciousness toward the likelihood of different moments in your life. Some of those moments you can prepare and plan for. Some you will toil with and dance around while deciding whether to engage or not. Still, others may be totally unexpected and come with no warning. This book will help you understand your moments, prepare for your moments, maximize your moments and give you the ability to benefit from this power. With the *Tempus Model*, you will begin to understand that this power is harvested in you, for you. After all, the moment is owned by each individual who comes face to face with it. Therefore, the moment is yours.

Time is the single common commodity that transcends culture, occupation, societies, career choice, and so on. It is one thing that everyone on earth possesses. Thankfully, we get to choose what we do with it. Since we don't directly control the amount of time we have, we are left to have significance in the moments that we do have. The point of this book is to help you examine your moments, prepare for those moments, and enact behaviors that are consistent with how you want to be as a person and as a leader. With that approach in mind, let's begin.

Chapter 2
THE STORY OF BRUNO

"A moment of choice is a moment of truth. It's the testing point of our character and competence."
—Stephen Covey

TIME AND MOMENTS of time are precious. We often don't really pay attention to its pricelessness until it is called into question. What if you encounter the end of your time or realize that your time is being cut short? It is so hard to wrap yourself around this and certainly something no one wants to really experience. What if it is abrupt, totally unexpected, violent, and/or tragic? For example, those who walked into the World Trade Center on 9/11 or boarded United Airlines Flight 93 had no way of knowing their time would end that very day. The same can be said of those in auto accidents, caught in the crossfire of a grocery store robbery, or facing the mortality of a loved one. In all of these situations, we are brought to the reality of the temporality of our lives and the moments that we have.

Throughout this book we will discuss the power of a moment and how each moment we face can potentially alter the trajectories in our lives. As authors, we each will be including personal examples of how moments have been influential in our journeys. We want to begin with one such story that we offer as a baseline for all discussion in this book. This real-life example in the life of a young Joe Balskus (one of the authors) provided a memory of courage and unselfishness in the face of adversity and enabled motivation for him to carry on, using the example of a father to strengthen his own life. As you reflect on the story and as we reference the commodity of time throughout your reading, our hope is that you will naturally gravitate to and reflect on the incredible value of the moments you have. That you will offer increased attention to moments in your journey and understand that how you show up in your moments can change the trajectory of life for you and for others.

Bruno's Story:

Joseph Bruno Balskus listened intently and spoke quietly into the phone. "Okay, Doc, I understand."

He hung up and looked across the room at his wife and four children who were sitting around the dinner table. As he walked toward them, he left the call behind.

"All right now, let's pray and give thanks for this dinner and enjoy Mom's wonderful cooking."

After dinner the kids went off to finish homework and prepare for bed, and Bruno stood alone with his bride as they washed dishes.

"Who called, honey?"

"It was the doctor who examined me last week for my annual physical and, well … let's sit down for this."

With tears streaming down their faces, Bruno explained to his wife that he had just been handed the biggest bombshell (and greatest challenge) of his life.

Bruno was a proud military veteran. At the age of 18, a mere 20 years prior, he was landing on Utah Beach as a part of the D-Day assault package. He didn't speak much of the war, but the effects of it were evident. One example was when he would slip off and sit in the car away from the noise of the Fourth of July fireworks. Yet, he was a proud American who loved being a veteran of WWII and who enjoyed serving as the commander of the local American Legion.

Bruno was a qualified scout with Company E, 8th Infantry. Having survived the Utah beach landings, his

THE STORY OF BRUNO

job was to obtain information concerning the strength, disposition, and probable intention of the enemy forces. He used maps and aerial photographs to locate enemy troops, and find suitable positions for maneuvers of his company. In official information transmitted back to headquarters, while on a scouting mission, he suffered multiple gunshot wounds just outside of Saint-Lô, France. His wounds were significant and when found, his company did all they could to stabilize him. They sent word by radio of his location for extraction. Unfortunately, it was going to take a while to get to him. Needing to move forward, his company left him in a barn with a grenade and an M1 rifle. They placed them carefully on a table for him. With the nature of his wounds, he likely wouldn't be able to use them, but they were there. If needed, he resolved that he would find a way to pick them up and use them.

Within a couple of days, Bruno heard voices outside. It was a German company passing by the barn. A lone German soldier, looking all of 18 himself, walked into the barn to see the young American lying on the table. The two made eye contact. Bruno silently prayed, clinging tightly to his rosary. As he prayed, he noticed the German kneel by the side of the table. After a moment, the German soldier got up, patted him on the shoulder, and silently walked out. "Alles klar. Neimand ist hier (All clear, there is no one in here)," he heard the German tell his comrades. With that, they moved on.

The following day, he was found by friendly troops. He was triaged by a medic and stabilized and then

15

eventually extracted back to a U.S. hospital for treatment. Two years later, with the war over, after multiple surgeries and still on crutches, an artificial bone in his right arm, he was honorably discharged and returned home to a small town in the Midwest. It was there he met and fell in love with a cute waitress at the local diner. After a year of courtship, winning her favor and that of her parents, the two were married and began life together.

"They found a lump on my neck and tests revealed I have acute lymphatic leukemia. The doc told me it is very aggressive and I need to start treatment immediately."

With those words still ringing in their ears, the two prayed and wept together and resolved they would do all they could to beat back the invader. Treatments began, requiring two four-hour train rides each month to the Chicago Veterans Administration (VA) Hospital, soon escalating to weekly stays, with only weekends at home. Each visit home was increasingly difficult, and physically it was plain to see the cobalt treatments—the best they had in 1963—were taking their toll and rendering little, if any, positive effect on the aggressive cancer.

Bruno made a decision to continue believing he could beat the cancer. He prayed and prayed but also "in his moment" decided he needed to prepare his family for life without him. As a result, he made the most of individual and family time. Conversations around the table became more engaging, and he purposefully spent time with each of the four children. Moments together were thought of as teaching moments.

One of his favorite times with me was attending baseball practices and having teaching moments after practice during the drive home. Another was what I refer to as "mirror" time when my dad and I were getting ready for Sunday church. As Dad stood behind me and combed my hair, he began what became a routine trend and started discussions that began with "I want you to remember." I was eight years old and unaware my dad was dying, but I do recollect Dad had a certain level of soft intensity in his voice during mirror time.

"Smile at yourself in that mirror, Son. You look pretty good. In fact, I believe you will be the most handsome young boy in the church today." He continued, "Son, I want you to remember that how you look on the outside is important, but how you are on the inside is even more important." With that, he would take his finger and bring it over my shoulder to point to my heart.

"What you have in here is the key to living a good life. I want you to remember that kindness is a good thing and if you are kind to others, it will make them feel good and make you smile ... I want you to remember that you live in a great country and enjoy the blessings of freedom. I fought in a war to keep our freedoms, and you should always fight to keep our great country strong ... I want you to remember that you should always work hard and give your best effort to whatever tasks you are involved with, whether it is school or sports, or helping out around the house ... I want you to remember that God is the creator of everything we have, and you should always thank Him for all He has done." On and on the stories and lessons continued during mirror time and the rides home from the ballpark.

The stories and lessons were wonderful and memorable but as the cancer progressed, mirror time and rides in the car diminished in number. Yet they were embedded in my mind. He never let my mom or anyone see him downtrodden or bitter about what he was facing. He never selfishly detached himself from his family or his role as an officer with the American Legion and other community involvement. He marched on and gave his all to the end. On one occasion during his last days, loaded with pain medicine he had saved up, he proudly marched in the Veteran's Day parade with precision as he made his way down the two-mile stretch of his beloved hometown.

On his final train ride back home, he returned with a Plexiglas box he had made in the workshop of the VA hospital. I had just won 2nd place in the local punt, pass, and kick competition and was given a new football signed by NFL players. It was time to receive my last lesson from Dad. Presenting the box in the car after arriving home from the competition, he said, "I made you this to put that football in and I want you to keep filling this box with wonderful accomplishments in life. Work hard, be kind, and always go to church." This was followed by, "I want you to remember that I love you." Eight months after the doctor's phone call, Bruno was gone. What remained were the impacts of the moments. Moments in the car. Moments in the mirror. Moments that left a legacy.

Bruno's story makes one think of and contemplate the fragility of life. Let us use this to frame the value of the moments that we do have. To appreciate the time that we have been given. Once we can value that temporal component, we are in a position to really understand and maximize the moments in front of us.

While not controlling the quantity of moments, you can consciously develop the type of person and leader that you want to be in all of the moments that you ultimately have. This you determine action by action, word by word, and yes, moment by moment. That means you get to determine how you are showing up in every situation. Notice, we didn't say you determine the situation, but the preparation (and reaction) to those situations are fully within your control. That is an exciting and empowering thought even in the face of an uncertain future.

As for the consequences, some are fleeting while others are consequential and will long outlive the moment and subsequent decision(s). Each is different and only you, individually, choose your reaction and determine how you will come out on the other side of the moment. Decisions will be required. Will you change as a result? Will you harden in response?

Notice, we didn't say you always get to choose the moment. You don't always get that luxury, as Bruno didn't with his diagnosis. However, one does choose the response, and that response could be a physical action. It could be a different course for your life, or it may consist of acceptance of the impact and how you are going to mentally and psychologically persist as a result of the moment. In each of those cases, nevertheless, a choice is still made ... and thankfully you are the one to make that choice.

Chapter 3

FOUNDATIONAL FRAMEWORK FOR MOMENTS: WHO DO I SAY I AM?

> "Time will say nothing but,
> I told you so."
> 		—W. H. Auden

YOU HAVE INVARIABLY heard the phrase "it only takes a moment." It is often used to reference something that we should be doing. For example, it only takes a moment to say a kind word. It only takes a moment to do the right thing. Or, it only takes a moment to make a difference. Conversely, it only takes a moment to slice someone with a curt or imperious word or to do an immoral thing when faced with common temptations. What is lost in the simplicity of the "it only takes a moment" phrase is the actual power and impact of the moment. Should we act or should we pause? Should we speak or should we stay silent? Should we walk away or should we engage? Each is consequential and has implications beyond the immediate moment. The reality is that we all have moments. Some we endure. Some we thrive in. Some we fail in. But, we have the moments nonetheless. The question before us, as it relates to our development, is "How will we utilize our moments?"

Moment is a word we are all familiar with. Our days and nights are made up of them. Some have caused us pain and others have brought us joy. Moments are a common denominator in our lives. We all have them. Yet, uniquely, we each get to choose how to spend them. They are a currency, of sorts, for our lives. When we string a series of them together, they create trajectories in our lives that create a force or vector for our thoughts, behaviors, and identities. The more of these we intentionally string together (as habits), the stronger the force can be in a certain direction.

These habits have power and can be utilized to influence specific outcomes. But what is also interesting about moments is that a single moment can impact that trajectory. Impact who you say you are. Impact the decisions you make. Impact what you stand for and how people view you. That places a significance on each moment that you experience. Let's pause there for a second. Read this intently. That means that these moments, each single moment, contains power. So, if you are heading in a particular direction, they can act as one more proverbial step in that direction. However, if you all of a sudden find yourself heading in a direction that you don't want to go or that is contrary to who you say you are, you can take a "different step" in THAT moment. In YOUR moment. From a developmental standpoint, this is extremely potent.

If we break down the individual components of a MOMENT, we can reveal how each component can enhance our understanding of our leadership performance. This is because while it is easy to hyper-fixate on the specific moment itself, the reality is that our resultant impact on, and effect of, the moment was set in motion before the moment actually takes place. Moments don't occur in a vacuum, they proceed from our previous thoughts and actions, and connect to future moments. This can be thought of as a chain of events. If you fail to understand the surrounding effects of how you show up to the moment, then you are necessarily missing the true impact the moment can have.

Now, it is easy to think of moments in a positive light. What we mean is that if there is a potential positive moment, and if you are aware of how you show up to that moment, you are in a position to maximize the potential impact of that moment. In other words, getting the most out of the moment. Athletes practice countless hours so that they are ready to perform their best in the moment they are called upon. However, the reverse is also true. If you are walking into a potential

FOUNDATIONAL FRAMEWORK FOR MOMENTS: WHO DO I SAY I AM?

negative moment with intentionality, then you are in a better position to minimize the collateral fallout from that moment on yourself and those around you.

As an example, let's say you are the leader of a team and you have an individual who is underperforming. As a result, you need to provide them with feedback about their lack of performance. There are many ways that you can approach that feedback situation. Some of those approaches will have a positive developmental trajectory. Some will have a negative trajectory. How you think about your approach ahead of time (preparation) will have a significant effect on the outcome(s) of that feedback moment. Not just for you as a leader, but for the individual, the team, and potentially the entire organization. While you may not be looking forward to the situation, the reality is that you have a lot you can bring into the moment to either lessen or increase the odds of a successful outcome for the individual as well as the team overall.

In order to understand and develop from our moments, we offer a model by which you can maximize the moments in your life. Understand that moments themselves don't have emotions or feelings. They don't necessarily have a prescribed consequence (good or bad). They are temporal. What you bring into your moments, or allow into your moments, is what impacts what you take out of the moments. You don't show up into your moments void. Rather, things come with you.

Sports teams don't show up to a game void or unaware. Their performance is the sum total of what they have done to prepare. How they have been coached, how they practiced, who is ready to play, who is unable to play, etc. Businesses don't show up to a negotiation without having fully vetted their position in addition to understanding the interests and motivations of those sitting across the table from them. An educator doesn't show up to the class period without preparing for the lesson and an awareness of what they want to cover with respect to the learning objectives. It is akin to what Benjamin Franklin was talking about when he said, "If you fail to plan, you are planning to fail." It is the notion that we can do something before the moment to frame the moment. To influence and impact the moment. That may seem very straightforward, and it is. However, if you think back to the moments in your life, has there ever been a time where, as you look back, you realize that you could have prepared better? Shown up differently? Chosen how to engage in the moment more effectively? While it is pretty straightforward cognitively, behaviorally it is not always so clear.

In the same way, we show up to the moments in our lives with whatever we choose to show up with, based on our preparedness. Pay attention to the word *choose*. Developmentally, that is powerful as we are not just a passive observer to the moment. We choose what we show up with. We do. We prepare. We plan. That is on us.

Examining the components of a moment presented us with the realization that there is a sequence one goes through, leading up to the ultimate moment of decision. As a result, we developed the *Tempus Model* as a sequential way to look at a moment. As the minute (pronounced my/'NOOT) point in time begins, many things are happening leading you to your confrontation with your thresholds. Broken down into the components, a moment consists of:

FOUNDATIONAL FRAMEWORK FOR MOMENTS: WHO DO I SAY I AM?

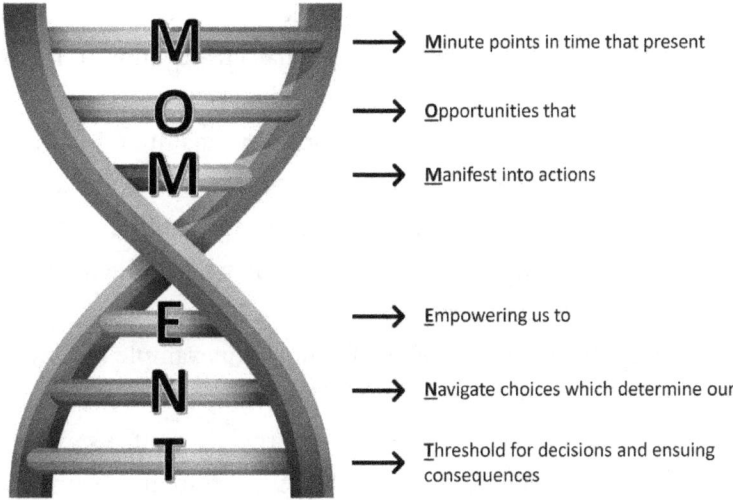

→ **M**inute points in time that present

→ **O**pportunities that

→ **M**anifest into actions

→ **E**mpowering us to

→ **N**avigate choices which determine our

→ **T**hreshold for decisions and ensuing consequences

The *Tempus Model* highlights that there are discernable aspects of the moment that we can engage in to impact the actual moment itself. Some of these occur before the moment. Some occur during. Some occur after. In all cases, we can thoughtfully consider these aspects and start to engage with them intentionally to impact our development. We will work through each of the components in the following chapters, but even with a cursory glance at the moments framework, we hope that you can start to pull out some of the specific aspects that impact the moments in your life so that you will be better able to navigate your choices which determine your thresholds for decisions and ensuing consequences.

You will notice that the model utilizes a helix design. There are several reasons for this. First, with the design, it shows that the aspects of a moment are connected in an intentional and structured way. By combining the six aspects (M O M E N T), you have a structure where you can see how they all link together. Second, this design also allows one to connect moments to create a behavioral chain that creates intentionality and stability in our actions. That stability, over time, can have a strong influence on our development and maintain inertia in our actions. Finally, connected to the idea of a chain, it allows us to home in on a particular moment to examine not only how we showed up to that moment but what influences impacted us in the actual moment.

Using the previous story of Bruno as an example of how to utilize the *Tempus Model* of a MOMENT, you can see we do not have to be victims "of" or just "in" the moment. As we previously mentioned, we choose how we will respond. Bruno hit a powerful threshold ... his impending death. In the moment of receiving his diagnosis, Bruno could have become angry, bitter, or withdrawn. All of which were choices. His decision, however, was to intentionally embrace the time (ultimately, moments) he had left and impart lessons and personal philosophies to his children.

So, for you, for each one of you, for each individual personality, for each "heart" being pointed to in this book:

- What will be your next moment as your continuum unfolds?
- What will you do to prepare yourself for your moments?
- How will your opportunities manifest into actions?
- Will you prepare and empower yourself to navigate your choices?
- Will your decisions challenge your established thresholds?
- What consequences do you want to achieve?

FOUNDATIONAL FRAMEWORK FOR MOMENTS: WHO DO I SAY I AM?

Life's journey, and one's development as a leader, is a process. In fact, it is a lifelong process that spans from youth to young adulthood to one's senior years. It is a complex matrix interwoven with one's upbringing, education, beliefs, moral compass, experiences, and other factors. What prepares you for such a time when you are "in your moment" of reacting to a situation? What techniques can you learn from those who have been "in their own moments" and have prevailed, emerging victoriously for resisting the temptation of wrong, evil, unethical, or immoral decisions? How can you prepare for the unexpected? How can you recover from a moment where you either weren't prepared or acted inconsistently with who you want to be as a leader? How can you prevail over perceived limitations that prevent you from meeting and exceeding your goals? These are heavy questions, but ones that we can start to dissect and understand in an intentional way.

Successful leaders are those who readily admit that self-improvement is a constant, perpetual, immutable motion in life. To lead, you must seek to grow, to analyze, to understand yourself, which then helps you to interact and lead others better. General Jim Mattis, former Secretary of Defense, highlighted this self-improvement mindset when he said, *"If you haven't read hundreds of books, you are functionally illiterate, and you will be incompetent, because your personal experiences alone aren't broad enough to sustain you."* While his words are quite direct (there is a reason why his call sign was "Chaos" and his nickname was "Mad Dog"), the point that he is making is that we all can (he would suggest must) and need to learn. That learning comes not only from our own experience, but the knowledge that others gained in their moments.

That learning helps us to develop the right mindset. Former NFL player and broadcaster Tim Tebow puts it this way:

> You need an elite mindset in the moment to be able to focus on the task at hand, to be able to have focus in the moment. And I would say it is one of the harder things in sports. I also think it's one of the hardest things in life. So many times, we let the moment, and the criticism, and the last play define the moment. We let the disappointments of yesterday, and the mistakes that we've made, the shame, and the guilt to define me in the moment so that I can't be my best in the present. Because I'm so worried about the last play. I'm so worried about the setback that I went through. Or, I'm just hoping that something goes well instead of being so focused in the moment.[1]

What all of this points to is the importance of preparedness and intentionality. We offer that learning leads to preparedness, which leads to showing up to our moments ready to engage. Our moments are significant to us and for our development. We must be careful to not allow our position or role (or lack thereof) to stand in the way. We must not think about leadership as positional, belonging solely to those in traditional roles of leadership. The reality is that we all lead, in different ways, in different domains. There are choices that we make that impact us and how we move forward. They can also impact those around us, no matter what our situation as a son, daughter,

---

1   https://www.tiktok.com/@timtebow_15/video/7296124634972359978

FOUNDATIONAL FRAMEWORK FOR MOMENTS: WHO DO I SAY I AM?

husband, wife, aunt, uncle, student, CEO, coach, teacher, military commander, or even President of the United States. You don't need a position or title to lead because no matter your situation, you are always required to lead yourself. The encouragement here is that we own that development.

Ex–Navy SEAL Jocko Willink has written on this notion of extreme ownership[2] and how individuals need to own everything in their world. Our idea of owning, controlling, and thriving in your moments is consistent with that notion. You control how you show up to your moments. We offer our model as a way to help you master that control. To be fully prepared for and present for your moments. To provide a foundation for this control and ownership, the next few chapters will unpack the individual components of the *Tempus Model*.

The important approach that we advocate and one that differentiates this book from the many other books on leadership and development is that we want the frame of reference to be YOU. Some leadership books or workshops featuring someone from an extreme job, an athlete, a CEO, a celebrity, etc., may offer beneficial, entertaining, and interesting information, but it can often be difficult to see yourself in their situation and translate that to personal applicability. While you may understand what they went through and the choices that they made, you are still left to "see" yourself in that situation or apply it back to your own circumstances. We are not indicating that this can't be useful for development. For some it is. The motivational impact of the message can resonate and connect people to the material in a powerful way. People are different

---

2   Willink, J., & Babin, L. (2017). Extreme ownership: How U.S. Navy SEALs lead and win. St. Martin's Press.

and different conceptualizations impact people in different ways. What we are offering is that for our approach, the power is in YOU, by utilizing YOUR experiences so that you can own YOUR development. In seeing YOU directly in YOUR moments. Seeing YOUR thresholds. Seeing YOUR opportunities. Understanding YOUR navigation. So that YOU can fully own YOUR decisions. So that YOU can develop in the ways that are important to YOU.

Chapter 4
"TYPES" OF MOMENTS

"Your words tell others what you think. Your actions tell them what you believe."
— T. D. Jakes

IF YOU PAUSE for a few minutes and think about the moments you have faced in your life, you likely have memories of the significant moments. Those noteworthy, relevant, impressive moments you can recall. You may have a positive childhood memory of a special moment with a parent, teacher, or coach. Or it may be a moment during a high school basketball game when you made the game-winning shot. Perhaps it was your first kiss at the high school prom. You may also have unpleasant significant memories, such as the death of a parent or loved one, a lost election, a poor performance report, a confrontation resulting in a divorce with a spouse, or a traumatic accident or event. The significant moments overpower the number of other moments that we take for granted each day. Even if we try to concentrate, we can't recall every moment we experience since the vast majority of them don't really rise to our awareness level or score a page in our memory book.

The fact is that while the majority of moments in our lives could be viewed as "insignificant," each day has the potential to present us with significant impactful moments. The question is, "Are you prepared to meet all moments and stand ready to face those that have memory-building significance?" Some, if we prepare ourselves adequately to face, will be controlled, while others will be ignored, mishandled, or uncontrolled. Unfortunately, you may also be presented with significant and unexpected moments, providing you no mechanism of control, regardless of how much you've prepared. Let's examine a few of the "types" of moments that we will encounter.

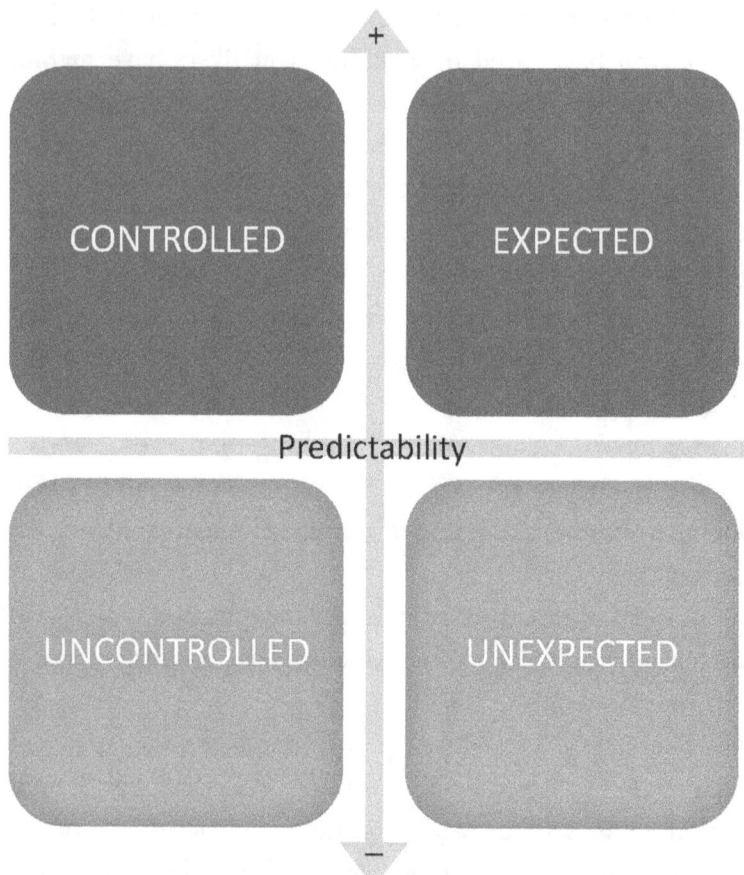

Figure A: "Types" of Moments

Controlled

A controlled moment indicates you have direct control over the moment itself and you can anticipate outcomes based on your preparation for the moment. It is always satisfying to see someone who experiences a significant moment in life they have controlled and orchestrated, resulting in happiness and total joy as it comes together. The outcome of such moments was the direct result of intentional engagement and executing a plan of action for the moment to come together. A marriage, the birth of a child, finishing a degree program, beginning a new business, landing a new job, or being promoted based on performance. These are events that have a significant impact on the trajectory of our lives. For example, finishing a degree or certification can have drastic implications on the types of jobs we are eligible for. This can have an impact on where we live and will likely have an impact on our financial standing. That is clearly significant.

However, while we may tend to think about the receipt of the actual diploma as the significant moment, the reality is that it is the culmination of a series of important moments that preceded it. The moments where we made the choice to financially invest in the degree versus other needs in our lives. The moments where we chose to study when we were tired. The moments where we made the time sacrifice to move our development in the direction we wanted to go. The old adage "Rome wasn't built in a day" is a testament to that point. It takes time (a series of moments) to build great things. Or from a long-term impact standpoint, it is as Benjamin Franklin said: *"An investment in education gives the best returns."* These moments tend to have a significant impact because of their ability to pivot our lives. It also puts added weight on them because we want to make sure that we prepare correctly for them and rise to the occasion. However, in each of the cases above, we have a degree of control regarding the overall outcome based on our intentional investment and preparation.

Finally, when we think about controlled moments, as leaders we have an added dimension. Those we lead also have significant moments. We need to understand that significance and recognize those moments to ensure that they are noticed. While a frontline supervisor on our team who just got promoted to a division manager doesn't necessarily impact us (or our development) as a significant event, it is highly significant to that individual both personally and professionally. It is the culmination of their investment and intentionality in their previous moments. The reality is that how we handle those moments can also have lasting impact on our teams and organizations. From an employment perspective, our response to their significant moment isn't just an individual response (from us), it also represents an organizational response as we are a leader in the organization. Back to the point about significant moments having weight, our response (or lack thereof) can have second- and third-order effects throughout the team.

We propose that these are controlled moments because we have direct control over how we show up to them and also what actions we take in those moments. Also, you can see that we have direct control over what we choose to do (the preparation). To recognize the significance or to stay quiet. To invest in our people, or to keep the investment for ourselves. From an individual perspective, these are the repetitions that we control and can help shape and define who we are as a person as well as a leader. From a relationship perspective, these are the repetitions that allow us to do things like build trust with others, develop others, encourage inclusion, create psychological safety, and create high performing teams.

Uncontrolled

Uncontrolled moments refer to those initially out of our control that often are caused or created by those other than ourselves. Oftentimes we actually believe we will be able to perform one way in an uncontrolled moment only to relinquish control and allow the moment to control us. There are also moments that we allow due to our own thinking and actions (or inactions). These can be particularly challenging to address because they often get to the core of how we see and think about ourselves. However, they need to be discussed as they can greatly affect our development and can be particularly insidious. Fortunately, this is another type of moment that we have an opportunity to influence, even if we can't overtly control it.

One way we can influence these moments is through our thinking. We all have scripts playing in our head about who we say we are or who we think we are.[3] Scripts are powerful because they impact how we see and interact with the moment. Simply put, they are instructions of a sort that give us direction on how we can navigate situations based on what we have experienced in the past. They provide information to us based on what we have seen in similar situations. They can have a powerful effect on how we react in the moment. For example, if my experience with customer service agents has been negative in the past, it is likely that every time I interact with a customer service agent moving forward, I may expect resistance and a negative experience. This not only impacts my reaction to the

---

[3] For more detailed information on scripts, please see: Schank, R. C. (with Abelson, R.). (1977). Scripts, plans, goals and understanding: An inquiry into human knowledge structures. Hillsdale, NJ: Erlbaum.

situation, but how I am likely to show up to it in the first place.

The irony is that I can, through my scripts, actually turn a neutral experience into a negative situation because I am bringing in my past experiences to corrupt my current situation. The negative affect that I show up with not only influences my thoughts and actions, but also all others involved. I can literally create a negative situation by anticipating one that would not have originally occurred. Going back to the example of the customer service conversation, how do you think I am likely to show up if all of my prior experiences have been negative? Without intentionally thinking about the moment in advance, it is likely to be in a way that could create the conditions that allow for one more negative experience (moment).

You are the author of these guiding narratives (scripts). Left unattended, they can grow and be impactful on our development—and not in ways you probably want. If you have tried and failed in the past, a script can remind you of that failure. They not only bring up what you said to yourself in that moment, they can also remind you of what others said as well. Left unattended, they can allow uncertainty into a situation and actually take control away from us. But remember, we control the script. We control those narratives of what we tell ourselves. We should not leave them unattended. Instead, we should be intentionally developing them to support our efforts along the way.

We can also have a tendency to oversample the negative experiences and under sample the positive ones when we recall things. For example, we may more quickly remember a moment where we didn't rise to the occasion (i.e., failed in the moment) versus those moments where we did. Therefore, in the moment, our unattended script can be feeding us information

"TYPES" OF MOMENTS

that may be factually correct (in terms of us remembering having not completed the action successfully), but doesn't always provide the context of where we did complete the action successfully. If left unattended, they can influence our behavior adversely. However, the great news is that you control the scripts. You literally write them for yourself. As you think back to your previous moments, has there ever been a moment where an unattended script exerted influence on a neutral situation, resulting in a less desired outcome? As you reflect on that, in that moment, did you also feel a lack of control?

To focus more on the uncontrolled part, let's think about the following example experienced by one of the authors (Balskus) and we'll call this the *water fountain* incident.

> The meeting had gone extremely well as indicated by the agreement around the table. Strategic issues were discussed, particularly in the areas of orchestration of events and assignments for everyone involved. At the conclusion, the commander asks for input from the group. "Are there any comments or concerns about this plan? Does anyone have a question regarding our approach? Does everyone agree this is the best way forward?" After a moment of silence, the meeting adjourns. Several of the team members gather around the water fountain, where one of the meeting participants begins to share thoughts on why the plan was ridiculous and would never work. "I can't believe the boss wants to take us down that path. I think the approach is destined for failure." A day later, the conversation is relayed to the commander.

What was assumed to be agreed by everyone in an open communicative environment has now been tainted by a member who didn't have the courage or professionalism to offer input in the meeting when asked to do so. The question at hand is, what are you going to do about it? This uncontrolled moment, left unattended, is threatening to drive a spear to the heart of what was thought to be a cohesive organization. You don't approve of it, and it is against the type of culture you want on your team. You have a choice as the leader to either intervene and correct the behavior or do nothing and just look at it as a one-off situation. The challenge with the second choice is that if you do nothing about that unacceptable behavior, you are tacitly allowing that type of treatment and behavior moving forward. You are saying that it is okay to agree in front of the boss, but in the hallway after the meeting, totally wreck the decisions that were made. You are, through your inaction as the leader, saying that you approve of that action and it is an acceptable way to behave on this team and in this organization. Is this really the message you want to give our team? Is this the culture you want to cultivate? Australian Lt. Gen. Morrison puts it this way: **"The standard you walk past is the standard you accept. If you're not up to it, find something else to do with your life."**[4]

Intervening and opening discussion on the inappropriate behavior can be uncomfortable and difficult but is often

---

[4] Australian Army HQ. (2013, June 12). Chief of Army Lieutenant General David Morrison message about unacceptable behaviour. Also see Sadler, A. G., Lindsay, D. R., Hunter, S. T., & Day, D. V. (2018). The impact of leadership on sexual harassment and sexual assault in the military. *Military Psychology*, *30*(3), 252–263, for more information on leader impact on organizational climate.

necessary, as was decided in this situation. Inaction would have resulted in many significant second- and third-order effects. Yes, these are hard and uncomfortable situations, but that is leadership. Even in a moment where you have no control you can still, through your actions, provide leadership in the moment. As a leader, you didn't encourage or approve of the moment in which the individual made the comment. However, you can create new moments to counterbalance the negative ones. For the individual who made the comment, you can create moments of clarity and accountability in what is expected from that individual and all members of the team. You don't take away the uncontrolled moment (the negative comments), but rather overlay it with intentional moments where you reinforce what you expect moving forward, thus creating clarity for future moments.

Unexpected

Not all significant moments are positive, and unfortunately, this can mean unexpected bad news. The loss of a job is one example. Often, there may be little or no warning that this is happening, and it will certainly have a pivot effect on our lives. An unexpected accident can be another one where, depending upon its severity, can cause us to live and experience life in a fundamentally different way.

As we think through the MOMENT framework, we can often be caught in a moment of unexpectedness. You likely are asking, "I can see how I can prepare for those moments that are planned, but that is easier said than done when it is unexpected." To this question, we answer, "We agree." In those situations, you only have control of what YOU do on either side of the unexpectedness. For example, many people put away money into savings or investments as a hedge against the unexpected. That doesn't take away from the effect of the moment, but it does create a different possible solution set on the other side.

Often, you can find solutions to overcome and even somewhat control the outcome of unexpected moments, but there are also those that are beyond the realm of control. In these moments, they impact you at your core and can cause you to approach life in a different way. These moments often result from a tragedy and can have long-term trauma on you and even those around you. They can occur at work or in your personal life. Wherever they occur, they are of such magnitude that they will end up impacting both domains. Often in these situations, you are left with questions such as "Why did this happen?," "Why did this happen to me?," or "How am I going to move on from this?"

Examples of such events are getting a critical illness diagnosis (remember back to the earlier story about Bruno), death of a family member, a spouse cheating on you, etc. These events rise above the normal day-to-day moments as their impact will leave a legacy on you. While we often think about legacy as a positive lasting impact, the inverse is also possible. When something tragic happens to us, it can shape us in an unexpected way. As an example, for those who are survivors of sexual assault, they are impacted at such a core level that it has a lasting impact on factors such as future relationships, trust, etc. The impact of that moment has a negative lasting legacy.

In fact, many of these situations may require seeking additional help through counseling and other support structures.

"TYPES" OF MOMENTS

These are not moments of our choosing. These are moments that occur that we are forced to deal with that we did not expect. Some have us questioning our morality. Some our faith. Some our belief in humanity. They are so significant that we just can't ignore these moments as they often consume our thought processes. The key to surviving these events is to understand our center and what is important to us. For many, this is their faith. For others, it is a strong support structure that will stand in the gap for us when we can't. For others, it is the support of professional help who will walk alongside us as we navigate a way forward, even though one may not seem possible at the time. All of these are mechanisms to help support us as we deal with the unexpectedness of the moment.

Expected

As leaders we don't get the luxury of not acting or letting someone else handle the situation if we are to fully embrace our responsibility as leaders. This even occurs when you come face to face with moments that you fully expect, yet even though expected, present challenges. Once again, it will be on you as the leader and you will have to show up. Even though you may be fairly certain how you want to act and how you believe you will act, you really can't be 100% sure how you will show up. Will you do what you need to do in the significant moments? Remember, failure to act is still a choice. Intentionally or unintentionally, your direct involvement will either occur or not occur. Are you adequately prepared for the expected moments you will encounter? It's easy to "think" yes, but not as easy to "know" yes. What are you doing to prepare for your significant expected moments?

IN YOUR MOMENT

The military will often use a version of a Leadership Reaction Course[5] to prepare officers for expected moments when working with teams. A team of 8 to 10 gather around a particular problem set. One person is selected as the leader and reads the mission card to the rest of the team. As an example, one might read:

> You are the leader of a unit that has been trapped behind enemy lines and you must get you and your team across the ravine to safety using the materials that are provided. The enemy is approaching and you have 20 minutes to complete the mission. All team members must cross the ravine to achieve mission success.

The clock starts and the chosen leader is theoretically going to take charge and direct the team, have them utilize the materials, and orchestrate a coordinated effort to get all the team members safely across the ravine to successfully complete the mission. As the clock begins to tick away, the supervisor of the exercise takes notes and later critiques the selected leader on what they did or did not do. In some instances, the chosen leader does not respond well and chaos ensues with no one having any clear direction. As time continues to tick away, you will often see a new leader emerge, and the selected leader will either relinquish authority and allow the new direction or dig in and refuse to let go of the leadership role. The former achieves mission success, while the latter typically results in exercise failure and a rather embarrassing debrief.

Scenarios such as those presented in the Leadership Reaction Course are simulations of real events that might occur

---

5   For examples of Leadership Reaction Course Tasks, please see: https://whfrtc.ky.gov/rangeops/training/Pages/default.aspx

in combat. They are performed in a condensed and controlled environment but actually present very effective and useful observations for the selected leader, the emerging leader, the followers, and the bystanders. What's really interesting is that the leader is often surprised by their performance and expected to perform differently. Some who felt they would breeze through the exercise are surprised that they failed miserably, while others who thought they never performed well in these types of scenarios were pleasantly surprised by how well they led.

Often a person known to the group as the timid or quiet one comes alive in the exercise and exhibits leadership no one ever thought they had. In a significant expected moment, the leader pulls on many things that lead up to action, or result in no action. What we expect or desire to do is sometimes overtaken by our training, our past experiences, our arrogance, our emotions, or our scripts. What shows up is a completely different version of what the individual wanted to be and felt they were.

You will see this play out often in your life when you observe somebody doing something, and you say to yourself something like "They should have seen that coming—it was so obvious" or "I wouldn't have done it that way." There is something fundamentally different about being in the moment and simply watching the moment. In the actual moment, even if it is expected, many factors at play will influence the situation. When you are on the outside looking in, it is easy to minimize the factors and simply focus on the event. Unfortunately, in life, you are not always an observer.

As you examine the above quad chart, the usefulness of it is not in the discrete sections, but in the ability to be able to think about different potential moments before they occur, and determine if you are prepared to be in the moment (even the unexpected ones). Generally, controlled/expected moments offer a high degree of predictability and you feel in control and able to sustain a modicum of balance. Conversely, uncontrolled/unexpected moments decrease our predictability, resulting in unsustained or interrupted balance. It is also important to note that these issues of controlled/uncontrolled and expected/unexpected are not mutually exclusive. There can be quite a bit of overlap between them within our moments. In our previous story about Bruno, he faced all of the different types of moments. For example, the time he was left on the table in the barn and the German soldier walked in, it was unexpected and uncontrolled. Let us share another example to explain.

Cole Lindsay (one of the author's sons) has dealt with gastrointestinal issues for his entire life. Starting at nine months old, he began seeing specialists to determine what was happening. Despite many doctors' best efforts, there didn't seem to be any clarity of what exactly was going on. In spite of over a hundred doctor visits, too many X-rays to count, dozens of tests, numerous hospital stays, multiple surgeries (operations on his colon, placement of a cecostomy tube, colostomy bag, etc.), hundreds of days and nights in the hospital, only pieces of the puzzle were slowly being unlocked (uncertainty and unexpectedness). Added to the mix were the multiple moves and switching doctors resulting from military orders, which impacted the continuity of care. After 16 years of various treatments and procedures, it was determined that about ¾ of his colon (large intestine) was not functioning and surgery was needed to remove it. The journey had been a long one for Cole, but finally, a definitive solution (expected) was found. He entered

"TYPES" OF MOMENTS

the hospital and underwent the surgery to remove the majority of his colon. The unexpected happened and he ended up needing some additional surgery to clean up some past surgery scar tissue, and it was also determined that a temporary colostomy bag was needed. Some expected, unexpected, and uncontrolled aspects, but Cole made it through the surgery. All seemed to be going well, but after a week, things headed in a negative direction (uncontrolled). It turns out that there was a leak in the stitches and his bowels were emptying into his stomach cavity. It was a large amount and had been building up since the surgery. It wasn't caught and his fever spiked.

The doctor said he had to have surgery immediately and that my wife and I "needed to say what we needed to say to Cole before the surgery." It wasn't a favorable situation and she wasn't certain that he would make it. It was unexpected and it was uncontrolled. It was one of those moments that as a parent you never want to be in. Something you couldn't expect and certainly something we hadn't considered. Potentially saying goodbye to our son as they rolled him to surgery is not something that my wife and I had ever thought to prepare for as most parents haven't. But, we didn't get a choice. This was where we were. He was being wheeled away for uncertain and unplanned surgery. After much prayer, and after multiple hours, Cole made it through the surgery.

After 25 days in the hospital and Cole losing 35 pounds, we were able to finally take him home. All four of the moments in the quad happened multiple times in that 25 days. Some we were ready for. Others we weren't. What we could control, we did. For what we couldn't control, we leaned on our faith. What was expected was prepared for. What was unexpected was survived. The reality is that the different types of moments don't occur one at a time or even sequentially.

Once again, we are back to preparedness and the lifelong, immutable process of our own leadership development. Are you coming to grips with this? It never stops. There are examples of great military tactical leaders who failed miserably in actual combat. There are examples of those who normally lived in the shadows of everyone else and waited to be told, who suddenly emerged in a pivotal moment, resulting in a Congressional Medal of Honor. In every domain you can think of, there are numerous examples.

The discussion above about the types of moments is not intended to be all-inclusive. Instead, it is offered as a way to think about how we can prepare ourselves for the different opportunities that come up in our lives both professionally and personally by starting to really think about them in a meaningful and structured way. There are likely many examples you have come up with from your professional and personal lives as you study the quad chart and read through the previous paragraphs. If you are thinking about those moments, that means you are starting to understand the significance of moments and maybe even how you can prepare to show up to them. It also starts to shape your thinking that not all moments are equal or necessarily going to help you toward your goals. But, you still decide how you are going to enter the moment and how you will choose to emerge on the other side of the moment. In that process there is power, and you own every aspect of that even though you may not control or expect the moment itself. With that understanding, you can now start to work through our *Tempus Model* and visualize how to show up for your moments better prepared.

Chapter 5

M
MINUTE POINTS IN TIME THAT PRESENT ...

"Realize deeply that the present moment is all that you will ever have."
—Eckhart Tolle

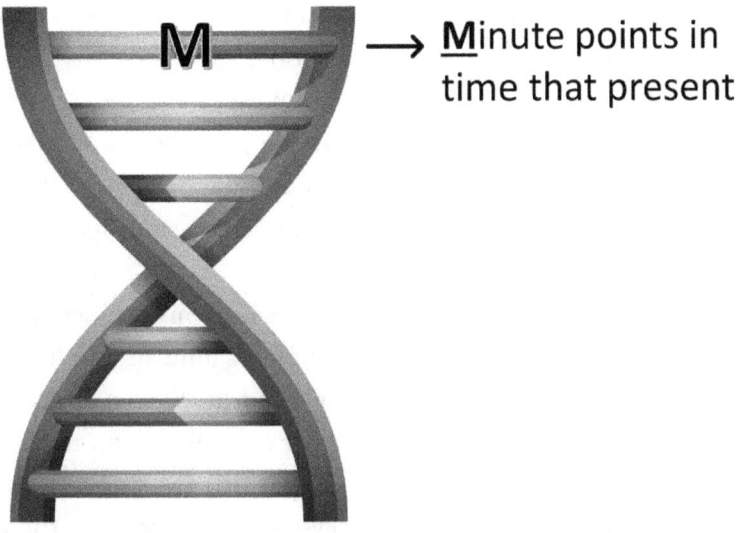

→ **M**inute points in time that present

WE HAVE PROVIDED a broad view of moments, and now it is time to break down each letter, to spotlight the specific and separate critical steps and components of the *Tempus Model*. The first entry into the model is the letter **M**, for "Minute (pronounced my/'NOOT) points of time that …" Here, we are thinking of a specific instance of time. That is because moments, by definition, are bounded within a temporal constraint. You can view them as finite, distinct units of time. While there is not a specific time frame on a moment, it is widely held that a moment is a brief unit of time. That means it could last as short as a split-second up to less than a few minutes. Anything longer than that gets away from the notion of a moment. As we have alluded to previously, even though moments are brief, it is important that you do not underestimate their significance.

This distinction is important as it allows you to examine behaviors in (and in response to) that specific period of time. If you think back to important events in your life, it is likely that you are recalling certain discrete periods of time versus days. This likely is what motivated Italian novelist and poet Cesare Pavese to pen, **"We do not remember days, we remember moments."** It's not that the days aren't important, it is just that the richness and fidelity of important moments leave significant impressions upon us.

As you begin to examine your behavior, this distinction is critical as it provides you with diagnosable units in which you can examine the prominence of the moment. From a developmental perspective, that is good news as it allows you to start to see the impact and influence of specific moments on your thoughts and actions. It also allows you to prepare for those moments.

It is also important to realize that while we are talking about discrete segments of time, those segments are necessarily connected to a larger context. They do not occur in a vacuum. This connection is important because the context contains certain conditions that can make some factors more salient than others. If you think about military service, for example, a moment that occurs in garrison (at a base during peacetime) or in training has a significantly different contextual loading than a moment that occurs when deployed in a war zone. The placement of that moment in a contextual space has meaning and can necessarily limit the solution set possible (or thought possible). It also can impact the preparation needed for that moment.

To follow our example, even though a military service member goes through such events as Basic Military Training and various other technical programs that prepare them for military service, there is a host of other training, education, and development that will occur prior to them deploying to a war zone. For one of the authors (Lindsay), prior to deployment to Kabul, Afghanistan, during Operation Enduring Freedom, there were additional requirements for medical, education, cultural, physical, marksmanship, among a host of personal aspects as well (preparing a will, power of attorney, financial preparation, to name a few). This was in addition to the 18 years of active duty service that preceded the actual deployment. The key here is that the context in which the moment occurs is significant and consequential and can impact our preparation. This is certainly not unique to the military. Many other domains such as police, firefighting, and medical professionals have similar contextual implications that vary between training and implementation.

In addition, moments not only have temporal and contextual components, they also are influenced by an experiential component. Someone who is new in their career has a smaller sample of behavioral repetitions from which to draw to determine the appropriate course of action. On the other hand, a senior leader will likely have experienced many similar situations from which to draw. This repository of lived experiences can have an impact on what the leader thinks is (or isn't) possible in a particular moment.

As you start to examine your moments in depth, you must be careful to not "contaminate" the exploration of the moment with the subsequent outcomes as a result of the moment. The reason is that you will conflate the outcome with the moment. If you do this, you lose the fidelity needed to understand the moment itself to include what preceded it. In essence, you lose the ability to really understand the moment and what you did in reaction to it. Certainly, the outcome is important, but if the outcome is a result of the action in the moment, you must be able to separate these for your examination.

From a reflection standpoint, this is critical. For example, we know that reflection is a key component to development as a leader.[6] You need the ability to look back on specific actions and thought processes in order to examine your actual influence on what happened regardless of the outcome or resultant implications.

> *We live in a world where it is so prevalent for people to look for outside reasons why they are where they are instead of looking internally and asking what hand did I have in this? Where did I fall short or miss?*[7]

That is how NFL Hall of Fame Quarterback Kurt Warner describes the importance of reflecting and understanding what is going on. The bottom line is that internal reflection is a preparatory step for our next moment.

If we go back to our story about Bruno, it is likely that he spent a lot of time in this reflective space. He didn't go down the road of "Why did this happen to me?" Instead, he was thinking about the messages and life lessons that he wanted

---

6   Densten, I., & Gray, J. (2001). Leadership development and reflection: What is the connection? *International Journal of Educational Management, 15(3),* 119–124, and Wu, Y., & Crocco, O. (2019). Critical reflection in leadership development. *Industrial and Commercial Training, Vol. 51, No. 7/8,* 409–420.

7   Warner, K., & Lindsay, D. (2019). First things first. *The Journal of Character & Leadership Development, Vol. 6, No. 3,* 49.

to impart. What were the significant moments that he experienced that he wanted to share? How did he want to prepare his children for the moments they would have in their lives? What did he want to do to maximize the moments he had left? How could he turn the moments lived into a legacy for his wife and children? That is reflection at its highest (and most selfless) level.

It is important to note that this does not just apply to negative inputs. While it is natural for you to focus on what you didn't do or what you did "wrong" in the moment, it is also imperative for you to spend time thinking about what you did correctly (or in alignment with who you say you are as a leader). Thinking only about the negative denies you the ownership and agency to own what you did correctly. Focusing only on the negative impacts your identity development, as you won't be able to gain the self-efficacy needed to continue to develop as a leader without additionally understanding the positive inputs and preparation.

One of the things that we have noticed in our numerous years coaching clients up through the C-Suite is that when examining 360-degree feedback, there is a tendency for the feedback recipient to want to bypass the positive (or supportive) feedback and jump right into the developmental (or perceived negative) feedback. This is understandable, but limiting to our holistic development. Maybe you have done something similar with your feedback.

Here's the challenge with such an approach. If you tend to focus on the negative and ignore the positive, then you are oversampling the negative feedback and giving it more weight. In other words, you are making the assumption (explicitly or implicitly) that this is occurring more often or is more important. However, unless you really examine the prevalence of both supportive and developmental feedback, you can steer yourself in the wrong direction when trying to develop a plan for improvement. Understanding, from a developmental lens, of what is going right is critical for your development as a leader. It shows where you can keep "leaning in" and showing up for your moments in a way you want to.

As you can likely see from above, leader development must be intentional. Part of that intentionality is examining what needs work, but ALSO what doesn't need work (i.e., is going right). A failure of development would occur if as a result of the feedback, you stopped doing some positive things that were working because you weren't aware of them working. In essence, you weren't really paying attention to them. Through the MOMENT framework, you are able to look at positive as well as negative behaviors to determine their impact on the moment and your resultant development. This is all part of your development as a leader. It's a process. As author Barbara Kellerman reminds us, *"Getting a leadership education is one process, being trained as a leader is another process, and being developed as a leader is a third process."*[8] We must be intentional about those processes. With all of this in mind, you need to be specific about the moment, your input to the moment, and the outcome of the moment.

Your ability to focus on the discrete points in time is also important for a practical reason. Your days are made up of a myriad of moments. It would be impossible to examine each

---

8   Kellerman, B., & Lindsay, D. (2019). The Leadership System. *The Journal of Character & Leadership Development, Vol. 6, No. 3*, 60.

moment in each day in detail. There simply isn't enough time. When we refer to moments in this book, we want you to focus on those moments that have important influence on how you show up, how they change you, the decisions that you make, and the outcomes that result from those moments (i.e., your actions and how they influenced the outcome). This connects back to what we talked about in chapter 4 about the "types" of moments. As you move forward, we encourage you to start to think about how you identify and think about those discrete/minute points in time (the moments) so you can really do a deep dive on their significance in your development. The more specific you are, the more you can really understand what is going on and how that will impact your development.

Chapter 6

WHAT ARE MY POINTS IN TIME?

"It's not that we have a short time to live, but that we waste a lot of it."

—Seneca

WITH THE TEMPORAL understanding of what a moment is, you can start to develop a plan to truly notice the moments that are impactful in your life. Notice the language here. The "moments that are impactful in your life." We are not talking about every moment. The reality is that it is not possible to intentionally monitor every single moment of every single day. While every moment "counts" in our total time, not all of them carry the same weight. Your goal, at least one of them, is to be able to identify those moments that are impactful.

So, as you think about impactful, put some thought into what that really means. That is because moments can be impactful for many different reasons. Some of them are impactful because they:

- Tell you something about yourself that previously was unknown (a shortcoming or a strength).
- Help tie you to humanity (helping someone in need).
- Identify a threshold in your life that needs to be addressed.
- Identify a shortfall in your preparation.
- Validate something about who you say you are.
- Allow you to "test" your values and principles.
- Confirm something new.

One thing that we want to be clear on is that not all of the moments are impactful. Some of them are large such as getting promoted, graduating from a program, finding out you are pregnant, etc. Some of them are significant because of what they represent, like:

- A moment spent with your child reading a book.

- A kind word said to a coworker who is struggling.
- Giving yourself grace for something you did wrong or when you didn't rise to the occasion like you wanted to.
- Providing encouragement to someone who needs it.
- Being supportive to a player who missed a play.
- Supporting a teammate in a time of need.
- Providing difficult feedback to a subordinate because they need to hear the feedback for their development.
- Giving others grace after they made a mistake.

As you look at the list above, the term *significant* means different things, and that is part of the challenge that you all face regarding development. The moments above span a large amount of situations. What doesn't change, in all of those situations, is you. Your intent. Your values. What you stand for. Who you say you are. Your ability to make an impact. First, though, is that you must understand yourself so that you can address and impact your moments. That means understanding how you are showing up.

One of the authors of this book learned how to understand the value of giving a few minutes to acknowledge and appreciate those who work for you. The lesson was learned by a young Captain Balskus and was reinforced later as a flag officer. I had prepped my bride for the big event. It was a formal affair with a mess dress (formal uniform for a military member) for me and a formal gown for my bride. Arriving at the gala, the mingling began, and I noticed an opportunity to meet the senior officer and introduce my wife. A beautiful tactical intercept was orchestrated to successfully converge on the senior official. Perfectly positioned and achieving eye contact, the

WHAT ARE MY POINTS IN TIME?

introductions began. After the "Sir, my name is ..." and halfway into introducing my wife, the conversation abruptly ended with a pat on the shoulder and the leader's eyes already looking over the shoulder onto someone obviously more important. This quick pat was followed by an impersonal, "Young man, young lady ... Hey Bill, how you doin'!"

We were left standing without any introduction worth mentioning. The impression given and behavior exhibited by the senior leader would resonate throughout a career. I vowed that night to never make anyone ever feel the way my wife and I felt, and I spent a career ensuring we always took a moment to show we cared enough to give a few minutes for proper introductions. That moment, that minute point of time, had a decades-long impact.

Contrast this with a moment when I was now a two-star general in my first week at the Pentagon. During the transition, time was allowed to bring family members to show them the Pentagon, our office, and of course, offer a small tour. On this particular occasion, my mother was visiting and we were climbing the black marble stairs leading up to the E-Ring Glass Door section where the leaders of the Air Force had their offices. As we were beginning our climb up the stairs, I looked up and saw Four Stars coming my way, all by himself and descending the stairs. As the figure began approaching, I froze and noticed it was the Chief of Staff of the Air Force,[9] General Mark Welsh.

---

9   The Chief of Staff of the Air Force serves as the senior uniformed Air Force officer responsible for the organization, training, and equipping of 689,000 active-duty, Guard, Reserve, and civilian forces serving in the United States and overseas. As a member of the Joint Chiefs of Staff, the general and other service chiefs function as military advisers to the Secretary of Defense, National Security Council, and the President.

This time there was no attempt on my part to intercept but rather, in the moment, the General stopped on the stairs and introduced himself. "Well hello, General, I haven't seen you here before. My name is Mark Welsh, and who might this be with you?" I introduced my mom, and after a few niceties, he said, "Tell you what, I've got a few minutes. How about we walk up these stairs and I'll show you my office." I was stunned and my mother was in love! Here is the busiest man in the Air Force with a world of responsibility resting on his shoulders, and he takes a moment to offer the most incredible and personable interaction I had ever witnessed. What an example. Both exchanges mentioned above took just a moment, but left indelible impacts, albeit in different ways.

Think of points in time that will benefit from you expressing a genuine interest and when people chose to share their stories with you. Look for times when you can ask people to tell you about themselves. It's never too late to initiate a conversation and get to know your team members. From a reflection standpoint, you should ask, "How are you showing up to situations like these?" Perhaps just as important, "What types of outcomes are you receiving as a result of showing up?" You need to understand that while the moment is clearly significant to the one receiving the interaction, it should be significant to you as well, due to the impact that can be felt in the moment.

For another example, one of the authors (Lindsay) was a young Air Force second lieutenant set to receive his first annual feedback. I was a little nervous as it was the first time I had formally gotten feedback on my performance since I was on active duty. I was excited as I readied myself for the feedback and showed up at my superior's office at the appointed time

WHAT ARE MY POINTS IN TIME?

(actually, I was about 15 minutes early as I had been taught). At the prescribed time, I knocked on the door, entered the room, rendered the proper military courtesy (salute), and I was told to sit down. After a few seconds, the leader looked up. He slid a form across the desk and stated, "Lindsay, keep doing what you are doing. Please sign here that you got your feedback and you are dismissed." The feedback form was signed, I stood up, another salute provided, an about-face, and out the door. At first, it seemed like this was the best feedback in the world. *Yes! Perfect! That couldn't have gone any better.*

But, as the day wore on, there was an uneasiness. I kept running that sentence through my mind: "Lindsay, keep doing what you are doing." Such a simple sentence yet it resulted in so many questions: What specifically did that mean? How can I improve from that? What should I keep doing? Was there anything that I shouldn't keep doing? I only saw my boss about once a week and wasn't really sure what he knew about me. I was new as an officer; certainly there are things I shouldn't be doing. Did he even know what I was doing? Part of the time, I wasn't really sure what I was doing, at least not fully. What was initially a positive moment turned sour, because of the missed opportunity in the moment. You see, the leader missed the opportunity to make a difference. To have impact. To pour into that young lieutenant. To amplify what was going well and to correct some things. The leader failed to show up in the moment and the lieutenant paid the proverbial price.

Part of the frustration was that it was not a competence issue from the leader. It was apathy, which has no place in leadership. That minute point in time was significant and the leader wasted it. They didn't recognize the significance of the moment and they squandered it. Much like the previous example of the two interactions, that moment left an indelible mark. The question for all of us is, "Are we recognizing the significant moments?" Not just for ourselves, but for those around us as well. If we aren't, then what are we willing to do about it? What can we integrate into our preparation to make sure we aren't missing out on those moments?

More examples can be pulled from our everyday personal lives, such as a moment spent with your child reading a book. At first blush, this may seem quite innocuous. Simply reading a book to your child. However, the way that one shows up to that moment contributes to the impact of the moment. Let's look at two different ways that you can "show up" to that moment. The first is one that is too often played out in families today. You are working all day, you pick up your child from day care, and you have to head home and tend to the nightly routine. You get caught up in the energy of the day and are rushing through the evening "responsibilities."

It is time to read a book to your child before they go to bed, and it is one of what seems like 100 tasks you must complete to close out the day. By the end of the day, the last few tasks are a bit of a struggle to get through. Instead of reading off and on with your child like you intended to, you read it for them as it will save time. You kiss them good night and the lights get turned off. Book read. Check. Child put to bed. Check. What is next on my list of tasks? That was an important moment. One that we failed to rise to. Instead of enjoying the moment, it was treated as a task and something else that we had to get through.

While we accomplished our mission of reading the book,

WHAT ARE MY POINTS IN TIME?

we missed our real opportunity. To be fully present. To enjoy the time. To ask our child how their day went. To make them feel valued and loved. To just be with them. To enjoy them. They were looking forward to the moment. Why weren't you? That moment should have been significant to you. Unfortunately, you laid down a behavioral repetition that you can't get back. It was an opportunity to love, support, and reinforce … and it was missed. You just didn't recognize it. It wasn't a grand event, but it was significant. It was important. The interesting part is that it wasn't something that you had to go out of your way to do. You were already doing it. You were already in the moment. You just didn't show up how you needed to. More importantly, how your child needed you to. While the circumstances may be different, can you relate to a missed opportunity to be fully present?

You have all the excuses in the world as to why, but the bottom line is you missed it. Developmentally, you need to make sure you have processes in place so that you don't miss out on these moments. To prepare so that you can be fully present in the moments that are significant. In the case that you occasionally do "miss" the moment, the good news is that you can fix it tomorrow. But, only if you recognize it today. What processes do you have in place to make sure you are showing up to your moments the way you want to?

The second way we can show up to that moment is intentionally. To show up how we want to. To take full advantage of those few minutes to pour into the interaction. To make an impact in that moment. To create a memory. To validate their importance. Much like Bruno chose to be present in each moment when he was talking with his children, so do we get to choose. The difference with Bruno was that he didn't know exactly how many moments he had left. The question for us to consider is whether "It's any different for us?" Does that make the moments less important if we have a few more of them? We would suggest not. Each important moment, regardless of the amount, is impactful.

So, how are you preparing for those minute points of time? How are you readying yourself? How are you reflecting on how you are doing? What are you doing if you realize you've fallen short of who you say you are or who you intend to be?

We would like to offer some questions for you to thoughtfully consider as you think about your "Minute points in time that present …"

WHAT ARE MY POINTS IN TIME?

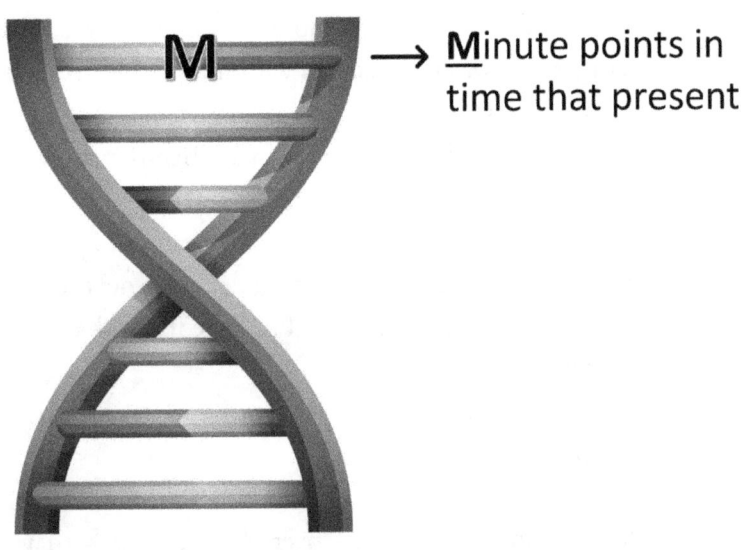

→ **M**inute points in time that present

Reflection Questions for "M":
Minute points in time that present ...

Take a few minutes to reflect on the following questions:

1.) As I look back on my development as a leader, what significant moments can I recall that shaped my approach to leadership?

2.) What is an example of a moment where I acted in a manner that was consistent with how I want to show up as a leader?
   - What caused me to act in a consistent manner?
   - How did I feel after that moment?

3.) What is an example of a moment where I acted in a manner that was inconsistent with how I want to show up as a leader?
    - What caused me to act in an inconsistent way?
    - How did I feel after that moment?

4.) What moments do I have coming up in the next several days that I need to make sure I prepare for so that I can be fully present?
    - What are those moments?
    - How will I prepare?

5.) What moments occurred over the past week that I need to spend some time reflecting on to support my development?

6.) What is a past moment in which I didn't show up the way I wanted to that I need to go and correct?
    - What happened in the moment?
    - What is my plan to "fix" the moment?

7.) What process(es) can I put in place to ensure that I am recognizing the important moments in my life?

Chapter 7

O
OPPORTUNITIES THAT ...

"Here's your opportunity, now you've got to make something of it."
—Chris Hemsworth

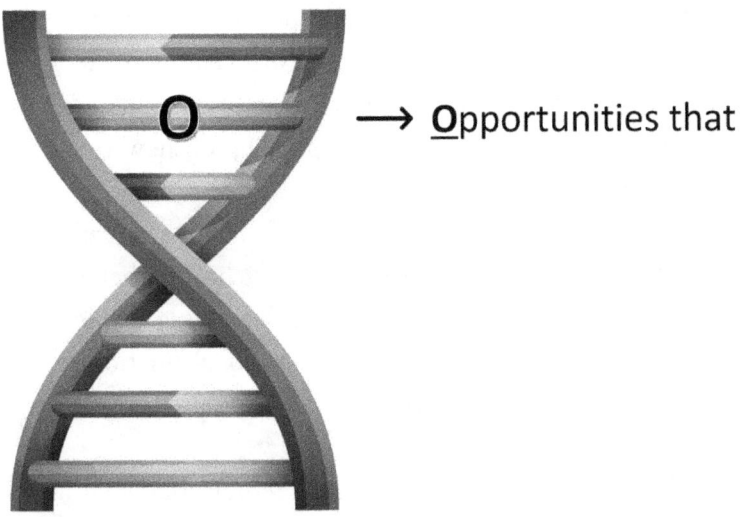 → **O**pportunities that

NEXT UP IS the letter **O**. Moments present **O**pportunities. Some of these will be positive and some of them less so. This is why preparation for the moment is so important. While some moments are predictable, as we mentioned previously, some will sneak up on you when you are not expecting them. As an example, for those of you with children, think back to the moment when you found out that you or your significant other was pregnant. For some who were trying to have a baby, the moment you found out about the pregnancy there was joyful confirmation in that news. For those that may not have been trying, the news may have landed differently. In both cases, however, the information that you received in that moment still presented an opportunity. While one was hoped for and the other was unexpected, it didn't change the opportunity that existed in that moment.

Another important component with opportunities is the

valence that we associate with the opportunity of the moment. What we mean is that there is likely also an emotional response that you can attach to the significance of the moment. Again, this can be positive or negative depending on how you interpret the situation. For example, let's say you hear in a meeting that your organization is going through a restructuring (not downsizing). That news inherently has neither positive nor negative implications. However, depending on how you perceive the event (our valence or emotional reaction to that event), it will have implications for how you process or react to that information.

If you are looking for a change in responsibility within the organization, that news could elicit a positive valence where you see the restructuring as a net gain event (an opportunity for growth). With the changes, that means there are likely some opportunities to move into different positions or parts of the organization that were previously unanticipated or unattainable. From this perspective, you could view the news as positive.

However, if you view the news as a potential threat to your status or position in the organization, you will likely take the information from a more negative perspective. Instead of thinking about what you can gain from the situation, you may be looking at what you could lose. This could have an impact on your status in the organization, your ability to have influence in different sectors, or even the path that you are on. From this perspective, you could see it as a negative event. As a result, you are likely to respond in a manner consistent with that negative perspective. As a leader, how might those different perspectives affect how you are showing up?

This notion of valence is important because it will likely impact your decision set and thoughts around potential actions and reactions. Questions to consider would be:

- Am I going to lean into the restructuring, or am I going to resist it?
- Am I envisioning what I can gain from this opportunity or what I can lose from it?
- Am I thinking about the opportunities it presents me for my growth and development, or am I thinking about what I am going to have to change?
- How can this be an opportunity for me?
- How am I going to message the restructuring to my team?

All of these questions are consequential, and the answers to the questions will impact how you behave with the information. You likely can think of specific opportunities that have arisen in your life (personally and/or professionally) that you could have viewed in several different ways. If you think back to the perspective you chose, why did you choose that particular one? Were there other events that were occurring in your life that affected your perspective? How did that initial perspective impact your behavior? It's likely that your "going in" position influenced your perspective on the opportunity that was presented in the moment.

It is important to note here that when you think about how you perceive the opportunity, that will necessarily have an impact on those you lead. If you see the opportunity as an area of growth, then you will likely pass that positive affect on to your team. If you approach it from a position of threat or loss, your team will also likely "feel" that affect. So, as a leader, you need to think not only how you will evaluate the opportunity, but also how you are intentionally (or unintentionally) messaging that opportunity to those you lead. They are likely trying to sort out the "opportunity" in their minds as well, and your reaction as the leader will have a significant effect in influencing their affect and resultant response. In either case, an opportunity still exists. It is just how you are going to utilize and maximize that opportunity for you and those around you.

With the opportunity being presented, you will be required to begin formulating your reactions to that opportunity. Unfortunately, the reality is that you are not always the one doing the choosing of the moment in the first place. In our earlier example of the restructuring, you did not have input into the restructuring decision of the organization but were the recipient of the decision (or as we suggest, the opportunity). Even though you didn't "choose" that moment, you still got to choose your response contained within the opportunity. You still own that decision process and how you will respond to that information. That is a subtle but very important distinction. In the moment, even if it is not an opportunity of your choosing, you still have the choice and ability to respond in a way that is consistent with who you say you are as a person and as a leader.

Remember, situations do not have affect. People have affect. It is the connection between our affect and the situation that is crucial. It is especially true when being part of a team or leading a team. You will likely be dealing with very different perspectives from team members. You need to make sure you are taking that into account when thinking about your leadership in that moment. Assuming everyone will "take" the information in the moment the same way you do is a mistake that many junior leaders make.

Speaking of "choosing," here is an example where an opportunity (actually two opportunities) was presented to one of the authors where a choice needed to be made. Cadet Lindsay was a sophomore getting ready to head into his junior year at the United States Air Force Academy. Between the academic years, the summers were broken into three three-week periods. During those periods, cadets were required to take part in different training or leadership programs. For one of these summer periods, I had been selected to attend a joint training program that gave future Air Force officers an appreciation of the U.S. Army by spending three weeks training, learning about and firing weapons, participating in small unit tactics, etc., at a nearby Army installation (Fort Carson, Colorado). It was an intense but exciting opportunity. Just prior to this program starting, I started dating a young lady from my hometown of Leavenworth, Kansas. Her name was Karina. She was visiting her grandmother in Colorado Springs for several months while her family was en route to be stationed in Brussels, Belgium, as her dad was an officer in the Army. While we had only gone on a few dates, and I know this will sound cliché, I knew that she was the one I wanted to spend the rest of my life with.

The challenge was that if I attended the training program, I wouldn't get to see (or talk) to her for three weeks and that she would be leaving the country to be with her family soon after I returned from the program. While I was certain in my feelings, I was locked in this program and would be leaving for it in about a week. I tried to move to another program that would allow me to see her in the evenings, but nothing was available. I had this fantastic professional opportunity in front of me, but I also had a personal opportunity that I knew I needed to pursue. After a week of being told no about shifting to another program, I had no other option but to go to the training. And, as a good cadet, I went.

The first phase was a 10-mile hike. It was designed that way to have folks really prove themselves. It was a rite of passage. If you completed the hike, then the rest of the program was downhill and much more enjoyable. Needless to say, I was not very motivated as I kept thinking about the opportunity I was missing by being away.

Every step of the hike felt like a step further away from what I knew I wanted. Further away from who I knew I was supposed to be with. Ten miles, with full gear, gave me a lot of time to think about the two opportunities in front of me. By the time I finished, and after much mental deliberation, I went up to the Army major who was running the program and told him that I did not want to complete the program. I was met with, "Why? You just finished the hardest part of the program. That was where most of the people were weeded out. You made it."

However, I definitely knew which opportunity I wanted to pursue. Steeled in my determination, I let him know that I wished to be moved to another program. I knew there were risks and there would potentially be some negative repercussions, but that didn't deter me. The Major got furious, and after many minutes of explaining (at high volume) what a loser I was, he stated the following: "Lindsay, if you quit this program, you are a loser and you will be a quitter for the rest of

O OPPORTUNITIES THAT ...

your life. Can you live with that?" That is some tough feedback to receive, at any volume.

The challenge here is that the Major only saw the opportunity of the program. He didn't see the opportunity of finding someone that you wanted to spend the rest of your life with, nor did he probably care. He just didn't understand the context. Sometimes, opportunities arise and we have to choose which path we are going to take. Sometimes they result in having to give something up in order to get something better. I was willing to take the heat in the moment and resultant discomfort because I knew what other opportunity was there. Was it a risk? Absolutely. I was put into another program that no one else wanted (ironically, one that I had volunteered for the week prior). I took a risk on Karina not feeling the same way. I took a risk at the opportunity not working out the way I wanted it to. However, I still chose. In the moment, I made a choice and stood by it.

You may be wondering if the risk paid off? After two years of dating, managing a long-distance relationship between Colorado and Belgium, thousands of dollars in phone bills (as there were no cell phones at that time), and over 30 years of marriage, it has. And, in case you were wondering, I didn't turn out to be a loser or a quitter as the Major forcefully implied.

The bottom line is that opportunities come in different types. They don't always come at convenient times. Sometimes they co-occur and we have to choose between them. Sometimes it is a choice between two good things, and sometimes it is the choice between what will hurt less in the long run.

Another important aspect of moments that is worth repeating is that opportunities are not all equal. While all moments offer opportunity, some will have a short-term effect, while others could impact the trajectory of the rest of your life. Think back to our earlier discussion on the "types" of moments and how that fits into our perception of, and reaction to, the opportunities that we face in the moment. What doesn't change, however, is the fact that you will craft a response that either moves you toward where you want to go, changes your goal, or moves you away from your goal.

Chapter 8
WHAT ARE MY OPPORTUNITIES?

"Opportunity is missed by most people because it is dressed in overalls and looks like work."
— Thomas Edison

THINK ABOUT SEVERAL commonly uttered phrases:

- If I had only done X, then things would have been different.
- If I had known that information in advance, then I wouldn't have made that decision.
- If I had only known.
- In hindsight, ... (enter any qualified excuse here).

Can you see a commonality in all of these sentences? All of them speak in some way to a missed or underutilized opportunity. Put another way, a lack of preparation resulted in an unrealized opportunity. The hindsight that we claim to have is actually our recognition of an opportunity missed. While initially that may seem like a bad thing, if one embraces learning from the "hindsight" it is actually beneficial long term to development. Because recognizing that you missed out on something allows you to take that feeling and turn it into something productive for your own development. The narrative on the other side of the moment may be something like, "I'll never do that again." While not enjoyable in (or after) the moment, it can drive you to be better. To let hindsight become your foresight and preparation. To show up differently next time. You see, as long as you have that recognition in the first place, it is a good thing. When you stop having that "hindsight," that is when you can negatively impact your development.

It is also common for people to look at another individual who recognizes the opportunity offered by the moment and refer to them as lucky. They were lucky because of X. Or they were lucky because of Y. In reality, often they were lucky because they were ready for opportunity. Seneca put it perfectly when he said, *"Luck is what happens when preparation meets opportunity."* This is not to ignore the times when someone is actually lucky. When something truly random happens. But, while you can't control every moment, you can control how you show up to every moment. You can actually impact your own luck. You may have heard the old phrase from Samuel Goldwyn, who said, *"The harder I work, the luckier I get."* Maybe it was that perspective and approach that led him to his vast success in the movie industry.

The problem with the notion of luck is that it doesn't reinforce the reality of work as it relates to development. The truth is that by preparing and working hard, you put yourself in a position to recognize more of the opportunities that pass in front of you. And it's not just that you recognize the opportunities, it's that you are positioned to be able to leverage the opportunities for your growth and development. If that is what people want to refer to as luck, then the good news is that you can influence your own luck.

For the truly random "lucky" things that happen, they can actually do more harm than good. What is the lesson to be learned from that randomness? You see, framing opportunities as luck steals from you the opportunity to learn and grow and replaces it with the fictitious notion that you don't have to work at something or earn it. It robs you of the ownership of development. Of leading yourself or others through the moment. It actually cheapens the value of the moment. While it may feel good short term, your long-term self is the one that is impacted.

The reason is that there is an elegance to earning something

WHAT ARE MY OPPORTUNITIES?

in life. To intentionally strive to get better at something. To think about it as Vince Lombardi did when he said,

> I firmly believe that any man's finest hour, the greatest fulfillment of all that he holds dear, is that moment when he has worked his heart out in a good cause and lies exhausted on the field of battle—victorious.

Those are powerful words and words that are hard fought and hard earned. What is your field of battle? Where is the space where you fight for your development. For some, it is the "fields of friendly strife" mentioned by Douglas McArthur.[10] For others, it is an office. Others, it is their house. The location is almost immaterial because it is how we show up, how we engage, how we battle (metaphorically) to be better in different areas of our lives. To be the version of ourselves that we want to be … that those around us need us to be … that we ultimately choose to be.

Some people get hung up on the words *victorious* or *success*. Many equate it to some tangible outcome like a promotion or money. When we frame it from a developmental perspective, it allows us to look at those two words in a more holistic and meaningful way. Think back to times in your personal or professional life where you were operating in a way that supported your development. Where was your focus? Was it simply on the promotion or the money? Or, was it in the investment of others? Was it the opportunity to serve others or serve yourself? The majority of leaders that the authors have interacted with

---

10   The full quote is "On the fields of friendly strife are sown the seeds that on other days, on other fields will bear the fruits of victory."

over the years (at all levels) share the notion that it is not the attainment of things or status, but the investment in others that truly made a difference both personally and professionally. Ironically, through that investment, the majority of leaders shared that the tangibles were a by-product of that investment and not the focus.

This isn't to suggest that we shouldn't be aware of our progress and what we are doing. To have goals and work hard toward them. We certainly should. What we are suggesting is that it is possible to develop and invest in others as well as see gains in our professional (and personal) lives. Unfortunately, the majority of us have at one time or another worked for a negative or toxic boss who saw the opportunity in their leadership position to take from others to strengthen their position. Remember what that was like? Remember how that felt? One of the things that always comes up when people are asked about what they like least about their jobs is their boss. Most of us can relate to that at some time in our lives. The missed opportunity by the leader to invest and develop others. Instead, they take for themselves and often leave a wake of disappointment and destruction behind.

We all have moments of opportunity that come up. How are you going to invest in those? How are you going to prepare for those? How are you going to respond to those? If you don't rise to the occasion, how are you going to overcome them? The power is in you to prepare for and to leverage the opportunity in the moment, moving you in the direction you want to go.

Some opportunities show up and look like they are heading in one direction only to change course partway through. Here is an example of an "opportunity" that could have gone

WHAT ARE MY OPPORTUNITIES?

several ways. As previously mentioned, one of the authors had deployed during their time in the Air Force. I (then Lt. Col. Lindsay) was sitting at my desk at the United States Air Force Academy in 2010 and was approached by my boss. He came into my office, closed the door, and said that he had something to talk about. Usually, conversations were had with the door open, so I knew this one was serious. He informed me that I was going to be deployed. I wouldn't say I was prepared for that moment, but it did happen to coincide with the surge of troops that President Obama had authorized to support ongoing efforts in Afghanistan, so I wasn't totally caught off guard. What was unexpected was what he said next. The real issue, my boss informed me, was that due to some personnel issues, I would be leaving in two weeks. That meant informing my family, offloading my day-to-day tasks, taking care of the myriad of tasks (medical, training, equipment issue, etc.) in only 14 days. Generally, an individual has multiple months to prepare, and prepare their family. Two weeks was not an ideal situation.

After a long conversation with my wife, who was incredibly supportive, the work began and I was on an airplane 13 days later. Limited preparation, but preparation for the opportunity nonetheless. The only thing that didn't sit well with me was that even though I got my orders and was moving through the process, no one could tell me where I was going to be assigned and what I was going to be doing while deployed. I was able to take care of the requirements, but still had no idea what I would be doing, limiting my preparation. After about a week of travel and waiting, I was notified as I was boarding the flight that took me into Afghanistan that there would be someone waiting for me when I landed. As I got off the plane, I was met by a sergeant major, who helped me with my bags and took me to where I would be working.

When I walked in, I met my boss and we started talking. It was clear after a few minutes that we were not tracking with what one another was saying. He was explaining what I would be doing, but none of it made sense. After a few more minutes, we found out what the problem was. The Army had a requirement for a position (the one they deployed me for). At that time, the other military services would often fill positions to spread the workload out. When the requirements for the position were translated from Army to Air Force, several things were left out. Essentially what happened was, they deployed me, at short notice, to fill a position that I was not qualified for.

Here I was, sitting in Kabul, Afghanistan, after a furious several weeks, traveling 7,338 miles, not able to fulfill the role that they needed. Let's just call it a big mistake. Once we both realized what happened, we were sitting there trying to figure out what would happen next. They certainly weren't going to send me home. I will admit with full transparency, in that moment, there were a range of thoughts and emotions that I experienced. Some of them were positive, some of them very much less so. But in the midst of that, I had a decision to make about the opportunity (not of my choosing) that was put in front of me. Was I going to lean in and make the best of it? Or, was I going to let the situation get the best of me? Regardless of the choice, the facts didn't change. I was deployed to Kabul, Afghanistan, for the next seven months. I leaned into the opportunity and it ended up being the single most impactful professional development experience of my career. If you put yourself in that moment, how do you think you would have

WHAT ARE MY OPPORTUNITIES?

reacted? Many of you may have had similar situations where you found yourself in the middle of a moment of opportunity and it was up to you to determine what you would do.

Think back to the many moments in your life that were significant to you where you leaned in and succeeded. Are those moments where you were lucky, or were they moments that were earned? That were toiled over. That involved struggle, perhaps. Whatever the conditions, they were earned—not because of what you intended, but what you did. It was you, within the moment, engaging intentionally with the opportunity before you.

We would like to offer some questions for you to thoughtfully consider as you think about your "Opportunities that ..."

IN YOUR MOMENT

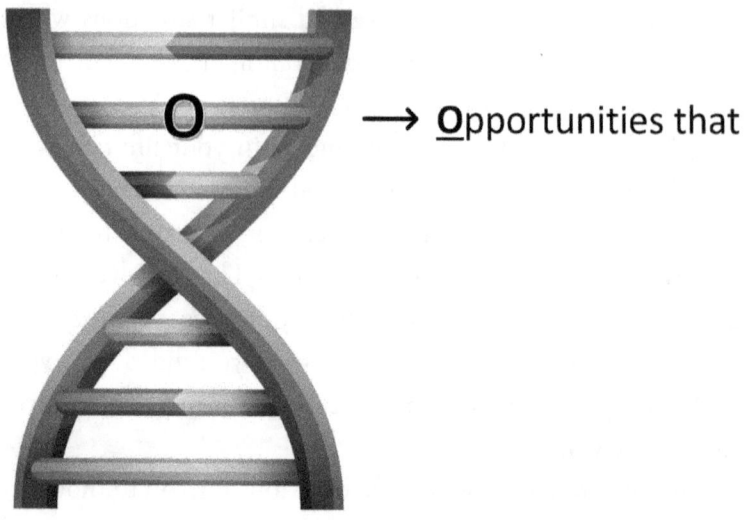

→ **O**pportunities that

Reflection Questions for "O": Opportunities that ...

Take a few minutes to reflect on the following questions:

1.) What are some moments (opportunities) that have shaped me to be the leader that I am today (positive and negative)?

2.) What are some moments (opportunities) that have shaped me to be the person I am today (positive and negative)?

3.) What scripts am I using that impact how I show up in the moment?

WHAT ARE MY OPPORTUNITIES?

4.) What opportunities do I have in front of me right now and how will I decide to act?

5.) Am I taking the time to reflect on opportunities to evaluate how I showed up and prepared for them?

6.) What do I need to do to make sure that I am showing up to the opportunities the way that I want to?

Chapter 9

M
MANIFEST INTO ACTIONS ...

"Manifestation is not about attracting what you want. It's about coming to the realization that you attract who you are."
—Dr. Wayne Dyer

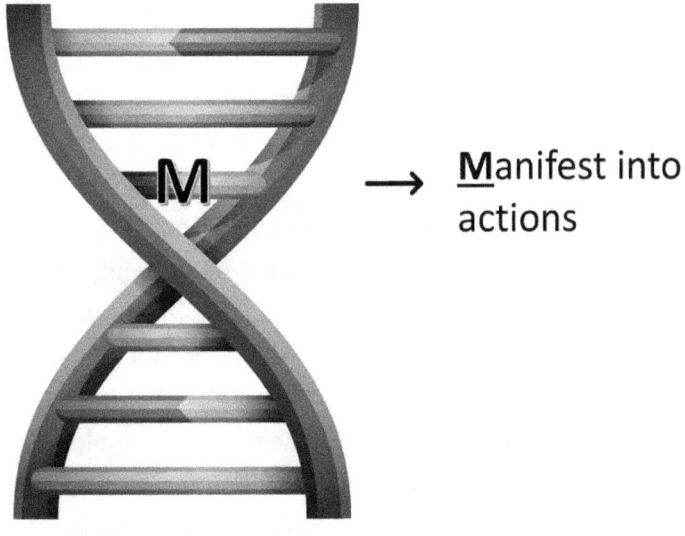

→ **M**anifest into actions

OUR THIRD CONTRIBUTOR to the *Tempus Model* is the letter **M**. The word **M**anifest is a common term today. You will often hear people using it with respect to trying to manifest good things through words, intents, and actions. Manifesting is a process that requires one to focus, to trust, and to exhibit an intentional level of dedication, based on what you really want. Therefore, manifesting is different for everyone, and we are all in a continuing refinement process depending on where we are at developmentally. The key to the word *manifest* is that it really comes down to demonstrating or making clear (in thoughts or deeds) how we want to move forward. It makes your opportunities and experiences a reality by changing your behavior. As it relates to our discussion, we are talking about what you are going to do "in your moment." What action(s) are you going to initiate? How will these actions affect your future self and all that is important to you?

Likely, what is going through your mind are thoughts such as, "It depends on the moment." or "It depends on what is going on at the time." or maybe even "It depends on the context." These are not incorrect and are logical questions. However, what they represent are reactionary thoughts. Each of those questions only takes into consideration the present moment. They don't integrate how we are showing up to the moment. The reality is that the possible set of actions that we are prepared to take are set in motion in advance of the moment through our preparation.

Perhaps an example would be helpful. If we look at many of the acts of failed discretion that take place (lying, infidelity, cheating, or other unethical behavior), we often tend to fixate on the current actions that are present only at the moment that the act takes place. We don't often take into account what happened prior to the moment. In the rare case that it is taken into account down the road, it is generally after the moment has occurred, the action was taken, and the consequences are about to be applied. In other words, there were preparatory steps that were taken that set up the conditions of the moment that created a set of predictable actions that were manifested. Those preparatory steps are critical when we think about development since it means that we have influence on the moment, even if we have never seen that type of moment before.

The good news is that you are in control of how you prepare for the moment. You can take control of this by asking yourself questions such as:

- What are my values?
- What is important to me?

M MANIFEST INTO ACTIONS ...

- Who do I say I am?
- How focused am I on my goals?

These are all preparatory steps to being able to boldly show up in the moment the way you intend to and to manifest the actions that you desire. While you may not have all of the specific details in mind when you prepare for future moments, that is okay. It is impossible to know with perfect clarity what will happen and when it will happen. However, you can set in motion (think manifest) a series of preconditions that can make it more likely that you will manifest the actions (or outcomes) that you want when called upon to do so.

Let's use cheating at work as an example. If you have in your preconditions that you are an ethical person, you have not only created habits around this but have also spoken that as part of who you are as a leader. You have as part of your identity as a leader that you will act a certain way. In this case, ethically. Therefore, when a situation arises at work (whether you have seen that exact situation before or not), you have an inertia for yourself around the idea of behaving ethically. So, when an opportunity arises to pencil-whip a form, or take a discretion that is not correct, you are more likely to behave in a manner that is consistent with who you say you are because you have taken steps to align your thinking with that behavior. Even if you have not seen that exact moment before, you "know" how you are likely to act because you have previously set in motion a series of events that support how you want to act in the moment. In other words, by thinking ahead of time about who you want to be, you have actually begun to manifest the type of response that you are likely to have, in the moment, based on that preparation.

Now, a counter to that line of thinking is that not everyone who prepares to act in a certain way will actually behave that way. Our response to that is that while that may be the case, the likelihood of acting in a consistent way is more likely based on the inertia that you have for yourself. Certainly, we are all fallible. However, by intentionally taking action that is consistent with who you want to be, you create a buffer from the moment. If you live according to ethical principles, have acted ethically in the past, and have aligned your leadership perspective around that, then you have created a pathway for yourself to continue that behavior even in moments that you cannot foresee. Therefore, you are less likely to be surprised by the moment and more importantly, unsure of how you should act. Therefore, you are more likely to manifest the behaviors that you want.

Sometimes, there can be doubts, inconsistencies, and troubles that can enter one's life that are causing friction which result in one behaving inconsistently. If you really go back and examine yourself truthfully through reflection, you can likely find something that had an influence and resulted in your inconsistent actions. While you may have acted inconsistently, and even caused yourself (or others) hardship, the important part for your development is that you can see that inconsistency and can correct your course—IF you take action. A single moment doesn't have to erase a legacy of investment. Even if you have to pay the consequences for your inconsistent manifested actions, you can still get back to who you say you are.

As we previously mentioned, the type of moment is not always in our direct control. Sometimes, unexpected things happen. While you may not always be able to prepare for every

M MANIFEST INTO ACTIONS ...

contingency, you will always choose an action or next step for how you come away from the moment (even if that option set includes a restricted range of undesirable options). That "choice" is critical to your development as you get to maintain some agency in the process, meaning you can have control over the actions that you manifest.

An important thing to note here is that while we are talking about manifesting action, failing (or deciding not to act) is still an action. You can choose to embrace and lean into the moment (often referred to as fight). You can run away from the moment (often referred to as flight). You can also ignore the moment (what can be referred to as failing the moment). This is a component that is lost on many new or inexperienced leaders. They feel that if they don't make a choice or take an action, there is somehow less accountability to the moment and its resultant consequences. However, anybody who has been in a leadership position for a while knows that this is not true. One's decision to not take action or to address the significance of the moment still has implications and, importantly, accountability as the leader. It doesn't negate the moment or the impact of the moment.

As another example, if you have as part of your leadership philosophy empathy for the people you lead, then that necessitates a certain set of expectations for yourself, as well as those you lead. It means that when something significant happens to one of your teammates, you don't have the "choice" to do nothing and ignore it. If empathy is a part of who you say you are, that necessitates manifested action on your part consistent with who you say you are. In short, you are implicating yourself when you make a stand about who you are as a leader. If you do not act in an empathetic manner, you are manifesting actions that are inconsistent with who you say you are. That disconnect between words and actions creates confusion to those around you. Confusion that you must still own as a leader, even though you may have chosen not to act in the moment.

This doesn't mean you will be perfect. As mentioned earlier, you won't be. It just isn't possible. The reality is that we can't expect our leaders to be perfect either. But, we do expect them to learn from those inconsistencies. Through reflection, to see what happened. We should be applying this same standard to ourselves as well. Why didn't we show up prepared for the moment? How can we show up to the next moment as prepared as possible? In other words, how can we manifest the actions that we need to be the leader we need to be for ourselves, our teams, and those around us?

Chapter 10
WHAT ARE MY ACTIONS?

"You don't have to be great to start, but you do have to start to be great."
—Zig Ziglar

THERE IS AN old maxim that states, "*If you want to see where you will be in 10 years, it will be based on two things: the books you read and the people you hang around.*" While it is easy to dismiss that as a bit pithy and simplistic, for those in an intentional process of development, it rings true. As we talk about "Manifest into actions," you must realize that effective manifestation requires work. You can't just sit around and think about what you want and expect it to happen. Even those who take a broader interpretation of what manifestation looks like still speak about "putting good things out there" in hoping to expect something back. The good things are our actions. Whichever conceptualization you take to the idea of manifestation, it still requires action and work. The work of leadership.

This aspect of the *Tempus Model* really gets at the input and the preparation steps. This is where the "why," the "what," and the "how" really come together. Through intentional investment, we broaden the aperture of what actions are possible. You can't manifest what you don't possess. You can't manifest beyond your thinking and belief. If you don't "see it," you can't "be it." Whereas some people hope that an outcome will occur without first putting in the requisite work, manifestation doesn't happen without intentionality, purpose, and, yes, work. Through your diligence you can create the conditions where the manifestation of your intended actions becomes a possibility. Which can then turn into a reality in your moments.

There is another common saying out there that "hope is not a strategy." There are many people out there who are hoping for something to happen without doing something about it. We are not suggesting that hope should not exist. Instead, we see hope coexisting with work which can result in the intended manifested outcome. Much like we talked about luck before, when you are in the process of doing something (like investing in yourself), you create the opportunity space for the thing you want to occur. That is how we see manifestation of actions.

So, let's look back at the quote that started this chapter: where you will be in 10 years will be based on the books you read and the people you hang around. Let's look at each of these. Why the books you read? It's because what you put in becomes the ingredients of what you put out or become. If you are putting in nonproductive material, you can't expect productive results. When world-renowned chef Gordon Ramsay is putting together a meal, he gathers what he needs ahead of time so that he can ensure that the recipe comes out the way he wants it to. He intentionally takes the time to source the ingredients before he starts so that he is prepared. If he uses inferior ingredients, this will necessarily have an impact on the quality of food he produces. If he is missing ingredients, then he has to fundamentally change what he is making and cannot expect the same taste or quality as if he had all of the required ingredients.

So is it with our learning. Think about these questions:

- What do I need to know?
- Where am I starting from? Where is "here"?
- Where are my gaps?
- Where can I get the information that I need?

All of this fits under the idea of "books that you read." What that is really talking about is your input. What are you putting

WHAT ARE MY ACTIONS?

in? How are you filling the gaps in your knowledge?

Let's say you want to play golf, but you have never played before or even held a club. The first thing you don't do is schedule a tee time and go out and try it out on the golf course. Not only will this be wildly unproductive for you, it will be infuriating to those around you. You could also start to form bad habits that you will at a future time have to unlearn. If you don't know what to do, then you need to find out how to do it. In this day and age, there are many ways to find out what to do. You could take a lesson (likely several) from a golf pro who can help you out. You could watch YouTube videos on how to play golf to gain a general understanding. You could read some books or articles about it that will walk you through basics such as the rules. The bottom line is that if you want to be able to golf, there are some necessary things that you need to do before you actually play golf.

The same is true with your development. You must know where you are starting from so you can fill in the gaps to improve your performance. A great place to learn this is from others. Otto von Bismarck put it this way: *"Only a fool learns from his own mistakes. The wise man learns from the mistakes of others."* When it comes to development, we require repetition (reps) to move us in the right direction. In some cases, these may be physical repetitions. If you want to gain more muscle, there will be numerous repetitions with weights that you must do. However, with things like leader development, you can also do mental repetitions. You can learn from what others did. Read their stories. Study the research. Reflect back to experiences that you have had (with prior leaders) to increase your reps. Think about it this way: there are reps you "learn" and there are reps you "earn." Most development has both kinds of reps, but you will need to determine the ratio that works best for you, depending on what you are trying to accomplish.

With this in mind, here are some questions for you (and all of us) to consider:

- What is the last book you read?
- What are your developmental reps?
- What are you putting into your life?
- What is the input in your life that is helping you to show up for the moments the way that you want to show up?
- How did it change and develop you?

By starting to ask yourself questions like these, you can really start to understand the developmental "food" that you are taking in and can really see how that is impacting you at the individual level.

The second part of the quote is the "people we hang around." This is amplified by those that you "consistently" hang around. This is an aspect that many people miss out on. The reason this is so important is because these are the people that will have influence on you or against you. When talking about development, you are talking about moving in a certain direction. This could be a direction you have already started moving in or it could be a fresh new direction. With this movement, you need to make sure that those around you are helping to create the conditions for success so that you can manifest the actions that you desire. Let's open that up a bit more.

WHAT ARE MY ACTIONS?

Think for a minute about the people around you:

- Who do I hang around?
- Who do I allow to influence me?
- Who do I get information from?
- Who are my biggest cheerleaders?
- Do I have any naysayers?

If you start to look at the above questions, you likely will start having some names and faces pop up. If you are wanting to develop, to really make some significant changes in who you want to be and how you are showing up, then you really need to think about who you have around you. To ask yourself if the people you are surrounding yourself with are helping you toward that end, or not? Do you have people around you that support your development? Do you have people around you who hold you accountable to who you say you are? At a basic level, who influences you?

One part of that has to do with understanding what we don't know. Ask yourself the question "Who is in a position that is in a direction that you want to move?" What we mean by that is that if you really want to move in the direction of being an effective leader, then you should ask yourself, "Who do I know that is an effective leader?" Then, once you identify who that is, work to spend time with them. If you are always the smartest person in the room, then you need a bigger room! How are you going to develop if you aren't learning anything from those around you? Who is pushing you? Who are you learning from?

We would add a third part to that original quote. It likely

won't surprise you what it is ... action. From a developmental standpoint, it's not enough to learn. It's not enough to surround yourself with people you can learn from. You must also be willing to take action and complete the reps on what you are learning. That is because as you learn and as you pay attention to those around you, you will need to personalize the experience in your own way. How will that learning be implemented in a way that not only helps you show up the way you want, but to also manifest the actions that you want?

You may have heard of the 10,000-hour rule that was introduced by performance expert Anders Ericsson[11] and popularized by Malcolm Gladwell.[12] The basic notion of the rule is that it takes, on average, about 10,000 hours to become an expert. Diving deeper, we find that 10,000 hours can vary based on what the skill is that you are attempting to learn. For our discussion, we want to highlight an important component behind the rule. It takes an intentional investment of time, over a dedicated span of time, with diligent practice to significantly develop in a particular area. To repeat our earlier message, if you want to increase the odds of manifesting the actions that you want, you need to be intentional, diligent, and dedicated. For those who have developed significant competency in a particular area, none of this should be a surprise. This same approach can be leveraged toward your development as leaders. The books read, and the people learned from, manifested into action.

---

11 Ericsson, K., Krampe, R., & Tesch-Romer, C. (1993). The role of deliberate practice in the acquisition of expert performance. *Psychological Review, 100*, 393–394.
12 Gladwell, M. (2008). *Outliers: The Story of Success*. Little, Brown.

WHAT ARE MY ACTIONS?

As with most learning opportunities, when you do the reps, not all of them will be perfect. Not all will be complete. You will fail sometimes. However, with development, you need to be able to give yourself enough grace to attack the next rep. Explicit in all of this discussion is the intentionality that you need to be able to invest the time to make the learning happen. Leadership author Josh Kaufman said, *"If you rely on finding the time to do something, it will never be done. If you want to find time, you must make time."* This ties into our earlier discussion of putting action into the equation of manifesting what we want. Without that action, without the repetition, without the failure, how can you expect to develop in a manner that you want and to manifest the actions that you need as individuals and leaders?

We would like to offer some questions for you to thoughtfully consider as you think about your "Manifest into actions …"

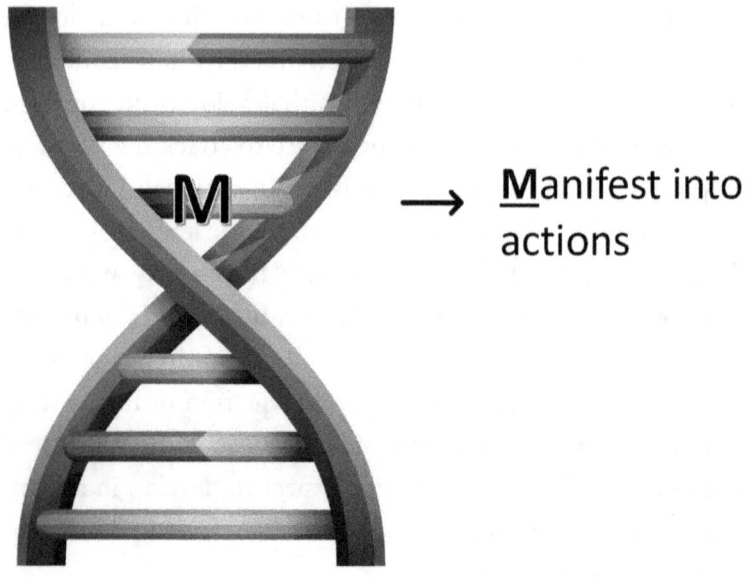

Manifest into actions

Reflection Questions for "M": Manifest into actions ...

Take a few minutes to reflect on the following questions:

1.) As you think about the manifestation of your actions, one thing to ask yourself is "How am I preparing for my moments?"

2.) Am I focused and clear about what I want?

3.) Am I correctly motivated to take action toward a particular goal?

4.) What input (books, podcasts, etc.) am I putting into my development to increase my knowledge?

WHAT ARE MY ACTIONS?

5.) As I think about the people I surround myself with, who is missing?

6.) Am I intentionally investing into my leadership development to manifest the actions that I want?
- If no, why?
- What is standing in my way?

Chapter 11

E
EMPOWERING US TO ...

"You must never be fearful about what you are doing when it is right."
—Rosa Parks

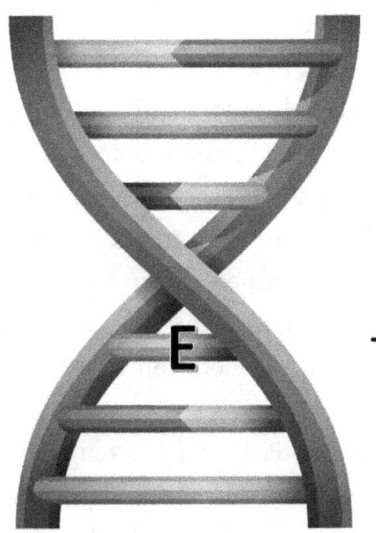

→ **E**mpowering us to

ON TO THE letter **E**. For those who have been **E**mpowered, it is a liberating feeling. Empowerment is a powerful, cogent construct. What it really means is that we have the authority to choose the vector of the moment. Is the moment going to move us toward, or away from, the leader we want to be or who we say we are? As we just discussed, our response to the moment goes a long way to help us manifest (through our actions) the type of leader we want to be. Even if the situation is one that we did not choose or that will have negative consequences, it still enables us to be who we say we are as a leader. To be transparent. To be authentic. To react consistently to our core values and beliefs. The moment itself does not change that. The moment doesn't choose that. We do, and that is great news from a developmental perspective.

Our choice in the moment is linked, to some degree, to our reactions in previous moments. What we mean is that you can have inertia in a particular direction. This can be toward the type of leader that you want to be or away from the type of leader you want to be. This inertia helps you build your identity. Creating consistency between your intent and actions allows you to confidently (think empowered) move forward and make choices with respect to that identity. To the degree that you allow yourself to stray from your purpose, it can introduce change and doubt into your thought process. This will also have the ability to move you away from where you want to be or who you say you are.

An important aspect of that inertia is that it strengthens your authority. If you are empowered to do something, then something occurs that gives you the authority to do that. For example, by getting a driver's license, you are empowered (under the legal terms of the state that issued it) to operate a motor vehicle on roads and highways. It doesn't mean that you didn't know how to drive before, but you have now been empowered (in this case by the state that you live in) to drive where you want. So, you see that sometimes empowerment comes from an outside source. Degrees from institutions of higher learning are another example of this external empowerment. With the advanced degree, one is empowered to seek jobs of increased responsibility and likely higher pay in the domain of effort you have chosen. As another example, military members are given the authority to utilize weapons, when required. Through their training, education, and rules such as the law of armed conflict, they have been empowered to wield deadly force when authorized and when necessary.

Concomitantly, you can also view empowerment from an internal perspective. The inertia that exists through your habits gives you a form of internal authority (or permission) to move in a certain direction based on your past actions. It is a confidence that you gain as you have "been here" before. Even though the details of the moment may differ, the shared knowledge of "I have done this before" or "something like this before" enables and empowers you to move forward with confidence in future moments.

Now, some of you may be saying that you don't always feel confident moving forward when you are in the moment. And, you are absolutely correct! You don't always have that luxury. But, just because you don't feel that confidence, doesn't mean you don't have the authority and are empowered to act. There are many reasons why your confidence might be lacking. For example:

- You may have chosen to act inconsistently in a previous similar moment.
- It could be that the impact of the moment is more significant than previous situations.
- It could be that you are new to your developmental journey.
- It could be that you are placed in a moment that is uncovering your vulnerabilities and you are too weakened to resist. What was suppressed as a speculation is now in front of you as reality.

However, even with that information in mind, that shouldn't keep you from leaning in and giving yourself permission to act. Development is uncomfortable. That is why many don't do it. That is why many try, and fewer succeed. But you mustn't let that uncomfortableness stand in the way of who you want to be or how you want to show up. You are empowered to act. You don't need someone telling you that you can. The bottom line is, will you give yourself the permission to act with empowerment?

Let's take a practical example of a woman named Mariah. Mariah decides that she wants to be more physically fit. She knows that in order to do that, she will need to start working out in some capacity. Previously in her life, she has inertia toward not working out, as that has not been part of her routine. But, she wants to change that and decides (gives herself permission and authority) to start a workout routine.

On the predetermined morning, Mariah wakes up and starts her new routine. Everything goes well that morning in the workout and she proceeds throughout her day. The next morning, as she gets up and prepares to exercise, she feels stiff and sore. Everything in her is telling her that it would be okay to take the day off. To rest and skip a day as she really should "ease into working out." That thought is the inertia that she has previously built up trying to keep her from working out. In that moment, in the wee hours of the morning, she has a decision to make about who she says she is. No one is standing in her way except for herself. No one is telling her she can't do it. After a few fretful minutes, she decides to get up and work out even though everything inside of her is telling her the opposite. She decides to act in a way that is consistent with who she now says she is (someone concerned with physical fitness). Every day, she makes that same decision empowering her actions, and before long, the consideration of not getting up is no longer an option because she has inertia toward the action that is consistent with who she wants to become.

This process of developing a new habit is just the first part, albeit a difficult part. As she continues her workouts, she starts to realize that doing the same thing every day in the workout is getting easier and almost automatic. She discerns that her body has grown accustomed to the workout and she is feeling complacent and bored. This is exactly where many people get in the way of their own development. They get started, develop a new habit, and then live in that habit for a long period of time. They don't continue to change or grow, and they settle into their new habit and form their new normal. Unfortunately, if you do this, your development will pause. You cease leaning in on your own development. Instead of building on the inertia that exists, you lean back and rest. You stop challenging yourself. Again, it is only you who stands in your way.

As leaders, this can be dangerous. Leadership, by design, is leaning in, not leaning back. If you stop pushing and stop developing, you are missing opportunities to serve your teams and organizations. So, you must keep pushing for your development. Dr. Anthony Hassan, CEO of Cohen Veteran's Network, puts it this way in terms of what leaders should do and be: *"The individual must have hustle. I need all team members (especially leaders) to grind with me on the work. I need passion for the work. I need integrity and transparency and someone who is not afraid of it."*[13] What he is referring to is not just the actual work of the team and organization, but also at the individual level as leaders. You must keep pushing to continue to develop as a leader. You need to

---

13   Hassan, A., & Lindsay, D. (2019). The hustle of leadership. *The Journal of Character & Leadership Development*, Vol. 6, No. 3, 86.

not be complacent or comfortable. If you do that, then you are not preparing yourself to show up to your moments prepared and empowered. In the long run, it will impact the actions you are manifesting.

We often see this in work situations. Many times we will see an individual pushing at their work. Working hard, developing their craft, and leaning into the work. As a result, these individuals are often promoted. The promotion offers an opportunity for them to contribute in a larger way to the organization. However, that contribution will likely mean they will have different responsibilities. With those responsibilities comes uncertainty.

At that moment, the individual has a choice to make as to how they will embrace that position. Will they rest in the success of the promotion, or will they keep pushing with the same impact that got them the promotion in the first place? In order to get to that position, they had to learn their craft and perform it very well. However, in this new capacity, they will have a different craft to learn. Will they take the time to learn this new craft with the same passion and vigor that they had previously? In that moment, they have been empowered to lead others. The organization has endorsed them for the position. But, where do they see themselves? Will they realize that, as Marshall Goldsmith stated in his book, **"What got you here, won't get you there?"**[14] That is a clarion call for all of us on our development. You must ask yourself, "Am I leaning into or away from my development? Am I coasting or pushing?"

The inertia that exists can also be in a negative direction if

---

14 Goldsmith, M. (2010). *What got you here won't get you there: How successful people become even more successful.* Profile Books.

E EMPOWERING US TO ...

you have failed previously. This ties in to what we mentioned earlier about scripts. So, it is understandable why you may not be currently leaning into your development. Fundamentally, you need to understand who you say you are as a leader. If you say you want to lead inclusively, that obligates you toward certain action. It also obligates you in terms of certain learning. What do you not know that you need to know? What do you need to do more of?

It comes back to how you want to show up as a leader. If you accept a leadership position, you have already obligated yourself toward the care and development of those entrusted to you. That is not an option. You took that on like you expect your leaders to take that on when they lead you. You must continue to move forward in your development. You have been empowered to do so and must move forward in that empowerment.

When we say we are leaders as part of our identity (and often our formal roles), we take on the mantle of development. What that means is that you, as part of your responsibility as a leader, must embrace the idea of lifelong learning. To embrace a growth mindset. To empower yourself to set a trajectory toward being an even more effective leader than you are right now. You obligate yourself to understand leadership in a more intentional and thoughtful way. You expect that from your leaders, and your teams should expect no less from you. The learning doesn't stop when you hit a particular level—instead, it intensifies. Dr. David Day, renowned leadership scholar and professor at Claremont McKenna College, puts it this way:

> *One of the things that you learn is that you might be a pretty good leader now, a 7 or 8 out of a 10-point*

> scale and you think you don't need to work on it because you have it all pretty much figured out. But we know, the farther you go and the higher up you advance in any organization, the challenges get more wicked and complex and you learn that it isn't out of 10 anymore, but out of 100 or 1,000. You don't want to be stuck at 7.[15]

That's a pretty powerful concept if you think about it regarding development not just as leaders, but as individuals as well. Where are you at on your scale? How are you different this year than last year? How are you investing in your development to make sure you are showing up to your moments prepared?

Remember, you have been empowered to be a leader. That empowerment may come internally or externally, but it is still there. Now, in this moment, you must endeavor to lean in and continue leading.

---

15 Day, D., & Lindsay, D. (2019). A lifelong process. *The Journal of Character & Leadership Development, Vol. 6, No. 3*, 69.

Chapter 12

WHAT DOES EMPOWERING MEAN TO ME?

"Don't bother just to be better than others. Try to be better than yourself."
—William Faulkner

FOR SOME, THIS idea of empowerment is a challenging one for a host of reasons:

- Part of it is belief.
- Part of it is doubt.
- You may feel that your habits are taking you in the opposite direction.
- You may not like where you are starting from.
- You may see yourself in a deficit position and are not sure where to start.
- You may see yourself in a difficult context.
- You may have just had a string of failures.

If you are thinking any of these now, or have thought them in the past, then welcome to the team! Those are the types of thoughts that precede development for those willing to take the first step or even an additional step.

Development is not comfortable. It is not comfortable because it generally requires change or a new focus. For an athlete, that can mean soreness from a new workout or routine. For a military member, that could mean moving to a different location for a position or training that is needed. For an academic, that may mean more focused work with respect to research or publishing. For those in business, that could mean adding a skillset that is needed for the next promotion. This applies to all domains if we want to develop. That is not a negative thing. Actually, it can be quite empowering to get a realistic view of exactly where you are and how you are showing up. That means that you must take an honest look at yourself and potentially admit that you are not where you want to be right now. That is okay. That is growth. That is our journey. That is what we signed up for.

The selection results came out and Brigadier General Balskus was to be the commander of the Florida Air National Guard. I was an Air Battle Manager by career field and had worked in key positions at the 125th Fighter Wing and at the state headquarters. As a leader I felt ready and able, but there was no denying I was to be the first non-rated commander of the organization, which included a Fighter Wing and eight other units of various mission sets throughout the state. This was uncomfortable and required me to address my approach to leading and interacting within a fighter pilot culture. I was in control of this moment and needed to act. My first meeting was with the fighter wing leadership, consisting of some of the best fighter pilots in the world and tremendous leaders in their own right. I walked in, the room came to attention, and I began. The air was thick with the unknown. The stares and concerns of the pilots were upon me: *This guy's not one of us. He can't possibly relate to us.*

I began with the history of the 125th Fighter Wing and how important and honored I was to be the commander of such an incredible organization. I then went into the great respect I had for each and every pilot who had ever flown and was flying now for one of the most prolific units in the world. Everything relaxed. Smiles and great eye contact were seen, and they realized my style was about them and supporting them and respecting the job they were doing. I couldn't be them and couldn't relate to the stories of life-and-death moments they'd had or the thrills they experienced from flying and being at the tip of the spear for America's defense, but I could lead them and have

WHAT DOES EMPOWERING MEAN TO ME?

their best interest in mind. That meeting was the beginning of a fantastic and memorable seven-year command relationship with an incredible organization.

As leaders, and as humans, we are constantly in a state of growth. For our purposes, it is acknowledging where we are, and that we want to move in a certain direction. That should be empowering and exciting for each one of us. The reason is that we have a direction that we can control. That understanding that we are in charge of the process. That should create a hunger in us to move ... to take action. If it doesn't, then it may require a little bit of introspection of the question, "Am I ready to develop?" Such a simple, yet powerful question. If we aren't ready, then what is standing in our way? Do you know what or who that is? If you do, what is it? If you are ready, then you need to set your plan, and start working on that plan. Former French football player and manager Arsène Wenger put it eloquently when he said this about putting your plan into place: *"Don't be scared to be ambitious. It's not a humiliation to have a high target and fail. For me, the real humiliation is to have a target and not to give everything to reach it."* And, you must remember, you are the one who gives yourself the permission and power to be ambitious in the first place. And, you get to set the goal.

Empowerment can come from different sources. As we mentioned previously, empowerment can be external or it can be internal. Let's look at those in a bit more detail. For the external, we can gain empowerment from the context or an organization around us. Let's examine an example from the United States Air Force Academy.

The United States Air Force Academy (similar to the other

military service academies) has an Honor Code. It states, "*We will not lie, steal, or cheat, nor tolerate among us anyone who does. Furthermore, I resolve to do my duty and to live honorably (so help me God).*"[16] That is the standard of behavior that is expected of all cadets who enter the Academy. That is a standard that is expected, reinforced, and when not met, consequences are applied depending on the severity of the breach. That seems pretty clear, and one can readily deduce why it is important for future military officers to have such an orienting code. If we are to trust future military officers with the use of deadly force, should the need arise, we must ensure that they hold a common set of principles and values so when they meet their moments, we know what their actions will be.

However, if we take a step back and understand that it is reported by the Educational Testing Service that somewhere between 75% and 95% of college students admitted to cheating (either while in high school or college),[17] then we have a potential disconnect. In fact one study by Dr. Donald McCabe, in cooperation with the International Center for Academic Integrity, indicated that 95% of the students they surveyed admitted to participating in some form of cheating. That was not a small study, by the way, as the sample was over 70,000 students.[18] As it relates to our discussion above about the Honor Code, this is important information for the Academy to have as they admit students from all over the United States. It doesn't mean that

---

16 https://www.usafa.edu/about/honor/
17 http://www.glass-castle.com/clients/www-nocheating-org/adcouncil/research/cheatingfactsheet.html
18 https://academicintegrity.org/resources/facts-and-statistics

they change the standard because of the students' experiences with cheating, but does mean that they must be aware of that information as they develop education and training programs to support life under the Honor Code while at the Academy. With cadets being admitted to the Academy from all 50 states, that means they are showing up with many different lived life experiences that need to be taken into account in the various training and education programs.

In fact, the Academy has utilized this information in their developmental approach. The mission of the Academy is to educate, train, and inspire men and women to become officers of character motivated to lead the U.S. Air Force and U.S. Space Force in service to our nation. To support this mission, they developed a leader of character framework[19] that focuses on three components that make up a leader of character. A leader of character is someone who:

- Lives honorably by consistently practicing the virtues embodied in the Core Values (Integrity First, Service Before Self, and Excellence in All We Do),
- Lifts others to their best possible selves, and
- Elevates performance toward a common and noble purpose.

You can see from those steps that they are providing a structure and framework where someone grows and develops into being a leader of character. From the above example, you can see the external framework set up to help develop

---

19 https://www.usafa.edu/app/uploads/21st-Century-LoC-Final-March-2021.pdf

cadets into leaders of character. However, simply looking at the framework and the Honor Code as a way to shape and norm behavior is too simplistic. We must look at the internal aspects as well. In order to be successful, the cadets must also want to be under the Honor Code. To live honorably. To not lie. To not steal. To not cheat. And to not tolerate those who do. It is not simply enough to have a Code. There must be intentional engagement in the process by both the institution as well as the cadets.

As it applies to internal empowerment, the good news is that you control this, you own this. This is you. Underscoring this good news is the reality that work and honesty are required to develop. People do not make you behave in negative ways. You choose the actions you will take. If you respond negatively, that is your behavior. If you are inconsistent with your actions, that is also your choice. From a synergistic standpoint, when you have a system set up to provide foundational developmental training and education paired with individuals who want to lean in on that development, good things can happen.

Whether you have a military academy, government service, nonprofit, higher education, business, athletic, or other organizational experience, you hope for an environment that is set up for you to become who you want to become or improve upon what you feel you need to become. Many take advantage of this environment while others do not. Again, you choose how you will engage in the system around you.

Unfortunately, you could also be in an environment that does not facilitate any aid to your development. In this case, the choice for your development still exists. Many will take

WHAT DOES EMPOWERING MEAN TO ME?

advantage of this situation and seek ways to improve and develop themselves, while others accept the conditions and do nothing and resign themselves to being a part of the environment they currently reside in. How regrettable this is—to allow the environment around you to determine how you will be and the actions you will take.

In either case, you still have a choice and the opportunity to grow and develop still goes back to you. Who do you want to become as a leader? What are you willing to do for self-improvement? Is your value system strong enough to accept where you are now and recognize that self-improvement shouldn't be a wish, it should be a constant pursuit?

Multiple factors affect how we empower ourselves to move forward. No matter what situation or environment you find yourself in, you must decide what you stand for. When Bruno took his finger and brought it over the shoulder of little Bruno and pointed to his heart, his emphasis was on the inside. The truth about what we are that is hidden from others. Bruno was creating the conditions for little Bruno to develop. But, it was little Bruno's opportunity to learn from that and apply it to his own life.

As discussed in the previous chapter on actions, what we allow into the heart from a developmental perspective is fueled by what we read, who we marry, who our friends are, who we have as mentors, who our naysayers are, our experiences, among others. You are well aware of your intrinsic values, and only you can decide what you do with them, within the moments you face and the opportunities you are presented with. Only you can decide what you stand for. Only you know where "here" is with yourself and if "here" is good enough or needs more development. If you are to gain empowerment, if you are to give yourself authority during this crucial stage of the *Tempus Model*, you must decide who you are and what you stand for, and own your empowerment.

We would like to offer some questions for you to thoughtfully consider as you think about your "Empowering us to …"

WHAT DOES EMPOWERING MEAN TO ME?

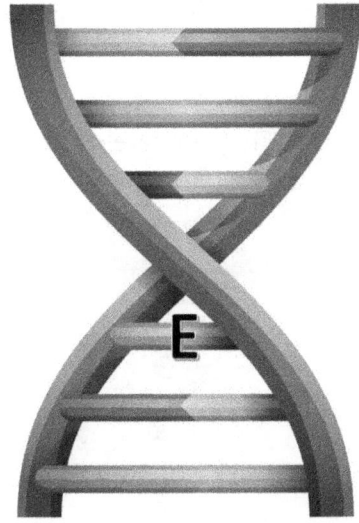

⟶ **E**mpowering us to

Reflection Questions for "E": Empowering us to ...

Take a few minutes to reflect on the following questions:

1.) Do you feel empowered to act?
   - If yes, why?
   - If no, why not?

2.) What is standing in your way of developing the way you want?

3.) What resources/training do you need to support your development?

4.) In what areas will you give yourself permission to develop?

5.) What are you willing to commit to your development?

Chapter 13

N
NAVIGATE CHOICES WHICH DETERMINE OUR ...

"It is our choices ... that show what we truly are, far more than our abilities."

—J. K. Rowling

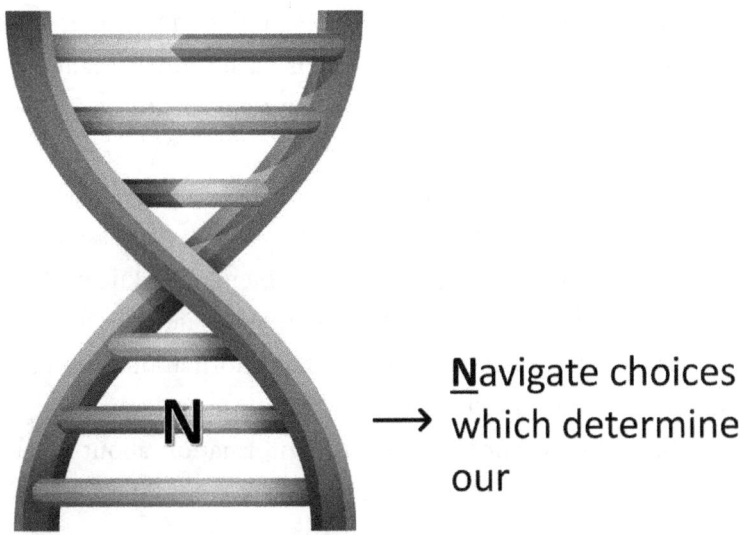

Navigate choices → which determine our

IT IS TIME for the critical and often overlooked letter **N**. Upon giving ourselves the authority to move forward, it's time to **N**avigate the choices in front of you and move forward to face the thresholds you have established. This is an incredibly careful, intentional, and pivotal step in the *Tempus Model*. Navigation involves ascertaining your position, then planning and following a route. In basic navigation we use longitude and latitude to describe our physical position anywhere in the world. In personal navigation, we plan and follow a route of choice that is ever evolving based on where we are developmentally.

Following this, the logical question becomes, "Where am I?" Not in the esoteric sense. But in a very real developmental sense. If you want to plan a route from here to there, you must know where "here" is and where "there" is. That may sound very simplistic, but many people aren't quite sure of where they are starting from, in a tangible sense. In addition, for many, they haven't taken the time to really codify where "there" is. Wanting to, or even hoping to, isn't navigation. It is really just wishful thinking. But it is critical that you start to nail down this notion of "here" and "there."

Anyone who has ever been lost on a trip knows the importance of "here." You may have caught yourself even saying to someone when describing your predicament, "If I knew where I was, I wouldn't be lost!" The encouraging news is that developmentally, you can always get that information. You have access to that feedback through many different sources. The challenge is that when you get the information about where your "here" is, you must receive that with a developmental focus. That is easy to understand, harder to actually do.

- "I don't believe that."
- "That can't be true."
- "They are wrong."
- "That's not how I really am."
- "Who said that?"

These are responses that executive coaches will sometimes receive when discussing an individual's 360-degree feedback[20] with them. If you look at those five statements, do they sound like they are being received with a developmental focus in mind? Of course not. That said, have you ever received feedback and had one of these statements (or a derivation of them)

---

20 360-degree feedback is a process whereby an individual can get feedback from different points around their position. This would include their supervisor, peers, subordinates, and others they interact with in their formal position.

come to mind? If we are honest with ourselves, we will likely have to say yes, at least to some degree.

We answer that way because there is usually a delta (difference) between how we want to show up and how we are actually showing up. This happens because the perception of our intention gets in the way of our action. Think about that statement for a minute. What I intend to do is not always the same as what I actually do. This is true of everyone. It is not because we are not authentic or that we are purposely trying to be inconsistent. It is because we are not perfect. It is a part of our humanity. Developmentally, that means that we all have work to do. Our choice is where do we want to buy into that development? Do you really want to know where "here" is versus where you may think that "here" is or where you want "here" to be?

From a leadership perspective, and due to the fact that we are all human, our leaders are also not perfect (as we mentioned previously). If we really think about it, we shouldn't expect them to be. If we ourselves, as part of our humanity, can't be perfect, then we can't expect our leaders to be perfect. What we can (and should, however) expect is to know what our leaders stand for and that they are always striving to be consistent with that stance. Moreover, we should expect them to study and grow as leaders. Incidentally, we should have that same approach for ourselves. Part of understanding that is to have the necessary feedback around us to close the delta of who we want to be and how we are actually manifesting that intent (as discussed earlier) to take care of the opportunities that present themselves every day.

To finish off the idea of that delta, the good news is that

the smaller you can make that delta, the more certainty you can have in your own behaviors. That certainty is important because those you are entrusted to lead can then count on certain behaviors from you. That provides security for them in knowing how you are going to show up today, tomorrow, and next week. That consistency also allows them to understand and contextualize behavior that could occur that is inconsistent with your stated purpose.

For example, if you say that transparency is an important part of your communication as a leader, then those around you know that is how you intend to lead. Because of the intent that you have verbalized, they can expect a certain level of visibility around your decision process. They should be able to see samples of your behavior that are consistent with that intention. In essence, they should see a pattern in your actions. If all of a sudden, there is a situation that occurs that does not have that stated level of transparency, based on your consistent track record of transparency, they are not likely to be confused. Instead, they are likely to see the situation as one-off and an anomaly since all of your behaviors in the past have shown consistency.

From a team perspective, that discrepancy is less likely to be disruptive as you have inertia around your transparency. This ties in to what we talked about earlier with respect to behavioral inertia and the predictability that it provides. It doesn't mean that they might not have questions or seek to understand the discrepancy. But, it does mean that, in that moment, the team doesn't fall apart. That is because the inertia that you have built for yourself and your leadership is transmitted to and embraced by the team.

An important component is that in that understanding of where "here" is, you need to make sure you aren't letting others unnecessarily determine that for you. While you need to have a realistic understanding of where you are at, you cannot let others choose that understanding for you. That exact situation happened to one of the authors (Lindsay) after retiring from the Air Force.

In 2014, after 22 years of service, I decided it was time to retire from the military. During the transition process from the military, I applied for a job at Pennsylvania State University that involved establishing a Master's Degree program in Leadership. During the interview process, a senior tenured professor who was on the selection committee took umbrage with the fact that I'd only had my PhD for six years. When I applied, I was 45 years old, had received my PhD in 2008, and was a full professor on the faculty of the Air Force Academy with over a decade of graduate and undergraduate teaching experience at multiple universities. I exceeded all of the requirements that they were looking for.

It turns out they were looking for someone with more "experience," I found out later. During the interview he said, "I can see that you have only had your PhD for six years. That will likely inhibit your experience and expertise in the field and would likely limit your effectiveness in the position. What do you have to say about your lack of experience?" The uniformed and arrogant faculty member was making an incorrect assumption. He thought that only someone who'd had their advanced degree for a long period of time could handle the position. What he was doing was trying to define where "here" was for me. And, the "here" was simply not correct.

With a calm demeanor and as much restraint and tact as I could muster, I explained to the committee member how his assumption of my experience was not only wrong but he was misrepresenting what was actually needed for the position. In spite of the tense exchange, the faculty member was outvoted and I received an offer for the position. It seemed like I was able to make my case better than he could make his. Part of the reason was that I was crystal clear on where my "here" was related to my qualifications.

While taken aback initially by the questioning, a strong lesson was learned that day that was never forgotten. The lesson was that no one has the authority to define where "here" (or where "there" is for that matter) is for me. While you may still have room to grow and develop, others don't have the right to say what you are and limit what you are capable of. As leaders, that is a strong lesson for us as we are examining future potential. Do we have all of the information that we need? Do we understand the experiences that the person has been through? We need to make sure we are making informed decisions and not letting ignorance or bias impact that information.

As we continue our thoughts around navigation, we have been discussing ascertaining our position (knowing where "here" is). The other component is the planning aspect. For anyone that has led, you know that not every moment offers an unlimited solution set from which you can select. You can't always assume that you can choose a certain way to get "there." That isn't reality. Some moments offer limited choices. Think back to our earlier discussion around the "types" of moments. Some of the choices may not be good ones. In some moments, there are only negative choices to be made. Conversely, in some moments, there may only be positive options to choose from. The reality is that most moments have a mix in the solution set. This further amplifies the need to know where "here" and "there" are contextually. We will discuss more about "there" in the next chapter.

As previously mentioned, while you don't always choose the moments, you generally do get to choose an option (even though they may be limited). You certainly get to choose how you respond to the moment. That choice is important as it has implications beyond the present moment for your long-term development. Having to choose the lesser of two negative options is still a choice, although it may not seem like it while you are in the actual moment. You still have some agency in that moment. That is important to remember as you reflect back on the moment after it passed and why you made the decisions that you did. In addition, you now know that not making a choice is still a choice. Choosing not to act is still a choice, and you must come to grips with that if you are to continue to develop as a leader. If you think back to the story about Bruno, he made a choice. He didn't let life live him. He maximized the moments in his life. Even though his life was limited, he chose not to be limited and to pour into those around him.

Another important thing to remember is that your values and belief systems will impact your ability to navigate your option set as well. Let's consider an example. If you say that you are a leader of character, that implies something about what you value and how you want to act and be seen as a leader. It implicates you and allows people to hold you to a certain standard that you define and ascribe to your leadership. It means that you will do certain things (tell the truth, treat others with respect, etc.) and not do others (lie, steal, or cheat). Again, it is you that is setting those conditions. While everyone may have some implicit thoughts about what a good or effective leader is based on their experience, you still chose the parameters that you set around your leadership.

That identity that you set for yourself is not meant to be limiting. Instead, it gives you complete freedom to operate within the context that you set for yourself. Remember, you set those conditions based on who you say you are. That creates a protective barrier for you as to what you will allow yourself to do. It also gives others a predictable set of actions that they can expect from you as well. Not only does this create stability for your team, it also forms an accountability structure for you in two ways.

One, it creates a reference point for you to compare who you say you are to how you actually act. The delta between those two is your developmental need. It is the area that you, as a leader, need to invest in. It provides you feedback as to where you need to grow as a leader. That allows you, from a planning perspective, to see what you are willing to invest as well as where you need to invest. In other words, it provides a vector for your navigation. It also models to your team the process of development, and that development is a core function of leadership.

Second, it allows others to reference your actions in comparison to your stated leadership philosophy. The closer these two are, the more likely you are to have positive team and organizational outcomes like trust, authenticity, teamwork, and consistency. In addition, it creates the conditions for psychological safety for your teams. Psychological safety has been linked to such important outcomes as information sharing, satisfaction, learning behaviors, engagement, as well as improved performance.[21]

That consistency is important as it allows teams to really understand where "here" is for their leader. Not to define it for the leader, but to provide stability so they can know what to expect. There is power in that consistency. Hall of Fame football player Dion Sanders puts it this way: *"Moments that are consistent ... turn into monuments."* The message there is that our consistency provides certainty which provides predictability which supports accountability.

As you navigate your leadership development, remember, you not only need to know where you are going, but also where "here" is. That is your starting point for development. If you find yourself in a slump of development or if you have taken a detour in your developmental journey, the nice part is that you can always get back to "here" so you can formulate a plan and work toward getting "there." And, if you ever have a question of where "here" is, ask those around you (personally or professionally), and you are likely to get all the information you need.

---

21   Edmondson, A. (1999). Psychological safety and learning behavior in work teams. *Administrative Science Quarterly, 44(2)*, 350–383.

Chapter 14
WHAT DO I NEED TO NAVIGATE?

"The goal of leadership is not to eradicate uncertainty but rather to navigate it."
—Andy Stanley

IN THE PREVIOUS chapter, we talked about knowing where "here" is. A precondition for success is that our desire to know where "here" is be asked with a developmental mindset. We should be seeking to understand. To quote Socrates, *"To know thyself is the beginning of wisdom."* If we want to grow, then we must understand:

- What we stand for: our foundational values and beliefs,
- How we are standing: where we are at behaviorally or our current "here," and
- Where we want to stand: "there."

The beginning of that process is to do an inventory of what we know and what we need to know. This begins with questions such as:

- What feedback am I getting right now?
- What information do I have available to me?
- What information do I need?
- Where are the gaps in my understanding?

If you notice that there is information missing on helping you determine "here," then you must figure out how you are going to fill in that missing feedback. There are a host of ways to get that feedback, and how you go about that will be somewhat dependent on your organization.

For many, 360-degree feedback is an excellent way to pinpoint how you are showing up. The value of 360-degree feedback is that it allows you to get information from your superiors, peers, direct reports, and interested others. This anonymous, multi-rater information provides a wealth of information about how you are showing up to different groups. 360-degree feedback has been linked to increased self-awareness, increased teamwork, ability to identify training gaps, improved relationships, and increased productivity. With that information, and often with the assistance of an executive coach, you can start to triangulate where your developmental opportunities are.

For example, if you believe that one of your strong points is communication, but you find out from your 360 that your communication skills are not resonating at all levels of the organization, then you have identified a discrepancy that you may want to address. The nice part about 360-degree feedback is that you can really pull apart the nuances in your communication. To continue with the communication example, let's say that you get good feedback from your 360 related to your communication from your superiors and your peers. However, you get feedback from your subordinates' 360 that is just the opposite—you aren't communicating well in terms of pushing information down into your team. Understanding that, you can really start to target where you need to focus your development. It is one thing to make a general statement about needing to improve communication. It is another to know that your communication up and across the organization is good, but down to your team is not as effective. Therefore, utilizing tools such as 360-degree feedback can really help you to zero in on "here" so you can see your current position so you can start to figure out how to get to "there."

So far, we have been talking a lot about "here," and that is critically important. You must be able to objectively know what is going on so you can tailor your developmental approach to the right behaviors. So, when you experience your moments,

WHAT DO I NEED TO NAVIGATE?

you know how to prepare, what to look for, and how you can maximize your behaviors.

Once you have "here" nailed down, it is important to start thinking about "there." Where do you want to navigate to with your development? What is your goal? It's one thing to know the direction you are headed. It is another to know the route you will take. Still another to navigate that route successfully. Or, at least increase the odds that you will navigate successfully. An effective developmental plan starts with your point of entry, which we discussed above. The next step is to determine where you want to go. What is your target? What do you want to accomplish?

If we continue our topic of communication, what do you really want that to look like? Where do you want to be in 3, 6, or 12 months? Do you want to increase overall information flow? Is it transparency? Is it clarity? Is it the amount of information flow within the team? You need to be clear and specific about what your goals are. Otherwise, you could fall back into the trap of good intentions and say things like, "I want to be better at my communication." Or, "I want to improve communication within my team." Or even, "I want to have regular meetings so that we can make sure team members are getting the latest information." All of those sound good, but without understanding specifically what the target looks like, you will have a hard time determining if you are making any progress. If your intention doesn't turn into action (specific goals), then you have the possibility of making yourself feel better in the moment but not having any real impact on your development. As John Burroughs, an American nature essayist, put it, *"The smallest deed is better than the greatest intention."* We need to do something.

There are many different types of goal-setting frameworks. Our job isn't to identify which one is best for you. The reason for that is that you have to determine what process is going to accomplish your developmental objectives. For some, that involves detailed tracking and accounting processes that are monitored daily. For others, it includes weekly reflection where you replay the week and account for successes and missed opportunities. You can also develop SMART[22] goals. Or, you can sit down with a mentor to help plan your process. The reality is that the best one is the one that works for you, holds you accountable, and provides you with the fidelity of information that you need to determine progress relative to your developmental goals. The bottom line is to pick the process that will work best for you ... and then work that process purposely, consistently, and tenaciously.

Once you have that established, you can start to figure out what you want to put against those goals. What are your commitments? That is a key question because without commitment, this merely becomes an intellectual exercise. To use a simple example, let's say you are planning a car trip. You obviously know where you are starting (your "here"). Once you determine a destination (based on what you want to do and where you want to go), you can plan the route to get "there." You have your vehicle ready, you know where the hotels are, you have determined sightseeing stops along the way, calculated how long it will take, and you have budgeted appropriately. You have taken all of the preparatory steps necessary to have a

---

22 SMART goals refer to goals that are Specific, Measurable, Achievable, Relevant, and Time-Bound. Doran, G. T. (1981). There's a S.M.A.R.T. way to write management's goals and objectives. *Management Review*, *70* (11): 35–36.

WHAT DO I NEED TO NAVIGATE?

successful and enjoyable trip. However, if you don't set a date for the trip (commitment) and actually get in the vehicle and start to drive (action), there is no trip. Just a bunch of preparation that didn't get you to where you wanted to go because it is more than the preparation. There must be action, as we talked about previously. The same is with your development. If you don't take action on your intention as discussed earlier, you will not get to where you want to go. You simply can't.

You must be very specific about what you are willing to commit to your developmental goals. What are the specific actions you will take daily/weekly to enact the plan? What are the milestone dates on when you would like certain things to happen? Who is keeping you accountable to your developmental plan? How will you show up to the critical moments that happen between "here" and "there"? What type of reflection is needed along the way to see if you are achieving your goals? You need to be very specific about what that will look like.

It is exactly this point why many developmental workshops and leadership interventions aren't effective in changing individual behavior. A person may attend and they may be engaged with the content. They are likely even entertained. They could even feel good about what they learned. Unfortunately, if they don't find a way to codify the learning from the experience, once they walk out the door, it is overcome by events. What is their actual plan? What does tomorrow look like based on what they learned today? What behaviors will be different as a result of the workshop? What is being committed to the development? What is the timeline? How will they know if they are making progress? They go through all the work to travel, attend, and possibly even learn, but they must think intentionally about the next step.

Otherwise, it becomes a one-off event that often won't move the needle on our development. For the organization putting on the developmental opportunity, they won't see the return on investment if they don't take the time to pull it all together. Maybe you have found yourself in that same position before. Both of the authors have unfortunately had that experience.

If we know that development occurs over time (and we know it does), then our plan must occur over time. We are back to that notion of time that we discussed earlier in the book. How can you create a series of intentional moments (or maximize the ones that happen organically) that are impactful and help you attain your goals? You see, your development is ultimately about creating clarity. The more clarity you can create, the more certainty you can have that you are setting yourself up to be successful in the moments between "here" and "there." That intentionality may even help you to create new moments where you can be successful and work your development plan.

The bottom line is that you need to have an intentional strategy that will move you from "here" to "there" in the most efficient way based on what you are willing to commit to that plan. The absolute beauty in this process is that you (and you alone) control that process of development. It is not based on what others think. It is not based on what others do. It is not based on what your organization provides. It is solely and uniquely up to you. We hope that gets you excited about where you are heading and how you will navigate your moments moving forward.

We would like to offer some questions for you to thoughtfully consider as you think about your "Navigate choices which determine our ..."

WHAT DO I NEED TO NAVIGATE?

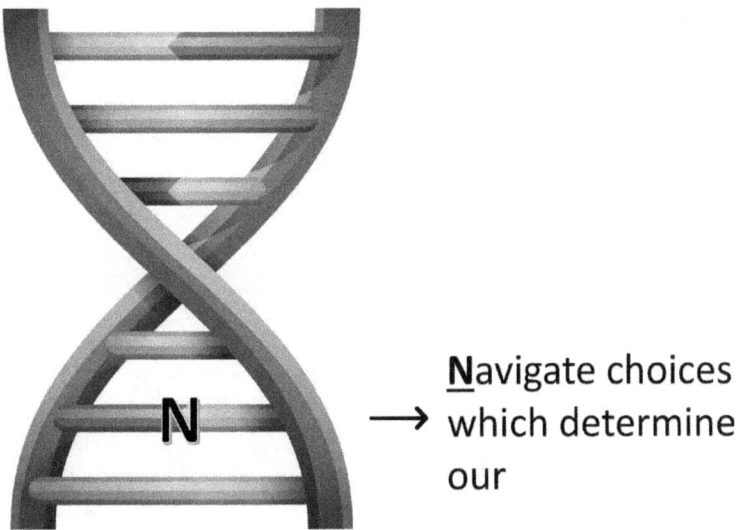

N → **N**avigate choices which determine our

Reflection Questions for "N":
Navigate choices which determine our ...

Take a few minutes to reflect on the following questions:

1.) Where is "here" for my leadership?

2.) What feedback do I need as a leader?

3.) How am I consistently developing myself as a leader?

4.) Where is "there" for my leadership?

5.) Who will I be accountable to?

6.) What is my timeline for development?

7.) What process can I put into place that will help me assess my progress?

Chapter 15

T
THRESHOLD FOR
DECISIONS AND ENSUING
CONSEQUENCES

"At this time, in this moment, roads diverge and it's on me to decide where I travel."
—Joseph Balskus

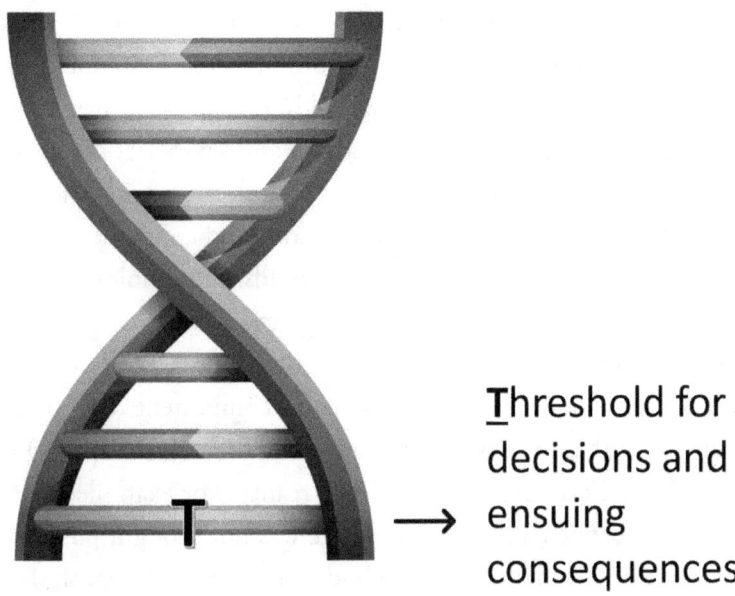

Threshold for decisions and ensuing consequences

IT IS NOW time for the final step in the *Tempus Model* as we unveil the letter **T**. It is here where you come face to face with your **T**hresholds. Will you adhere to the threshold? Will you level off? Will you disregard it? Will you break through a perceived threshold and accomplish something you previously felt was unattainable? What happens here will most assuredly and certainly have consequences, so you better have an understanding right here, right now, how you want to show up in your moment.

We have thresholds for pain tolerance, thresholds for what is considered right or wrong, good and evil, moral and immoral. We have thresholds for what we believe we are capable of or what level of time we can give to a particular effort. The fact is that within the moment, we invariably reach a threshold for tolerance where we stop, withdraw, or commit to go beyond our established but sometimes untested barriers. A point when our next step or decision starts the movement for something else to happen. We often set thresholds for exercising, drinking, eating, fantasizing, buying, spending, and saving. Some go so far as to set thresholds for personality tolerance with friends, family members, or spouses, supervisors, and colleagues.

The point is, we all have thresholds. Thresholds can be boundaries for keeping us from going beyond what we consider good behavior and can also be limitations that restrict pushing ourselves to new levels. An important component to remember is that the limitation (from a developmental standpoint) is often based on perception and not reality. For example, there was a time when a four-minute mile was not thought possible. It was thought that the human body could not accomplish that feat. Today, it is a standard by which some evaluate distance runners. Until it is done, it may SEEM impossible. Once it is accomplished, we wonder what stood in our way. From a physical standpoint, there are certain limitations that we face based on our fitness and capability. For example, no one is going to run a one-minute mile. From a developmental standpoint, however, we need to understand the permeability of the thresholds that we set. We are not limited by the same factors that we are physically. That is great news.

If we come face to face with one of our established thresholds and don't withdraw but rather move the needle forward, we must accept the ensuing consequences because our decision in the moment will assuredly result in consequences. Examples include:

- Blowing our budget.
- Becoming intoxicated.

T THRESHOLD FOR DECISIONS AND ENSUING CONSEQUENCES

- Dropping our diet.
- Giving up on getting an advanced degree.
- Exploding in anger with friends, family members, or a spouse and saying something we may later regret.
- We cross the line and move from an inappropriate controlled attraction to an affair.
- We let the drive for money turn to jealousy and greed.
- We make unethical choices to cheat, gamble, steal, or embezzle.
- We develop acceptable levels of caustic leadership behaviors from our own arrogance and pride.

It can even come out in our language such as, "I've had it." "If you say that one more time, I'm leaving!" "I don't have the money, but I'm buying it anyway." "One more drink won't hurt." "She's really attractive. One little rendezvous is harmless." "I just don't have the time to devote to an advanced degree." We can become so tolerant and accustomed to a newly adjusted threshold that what was previously unacceptable, becomes allowable, and our new norm. On the other hand, if we are so rigid on other thresholds, what was thought to be an achievable goal, becomes unachievable due to constraints or interruptions that we artificially place upon ourselves.

Once you find yourself on the other side of the moment where you made decisions at your thresholds, how are you different? Put another way, how did the moment impact who you say you are as a person, as a leader? Did you close the gap at all? Personal challenge questions can come from our analysis on the other side of the moment. Am I closer to, or further away from, my goal? What adjustments should I make to better prepare if this moment comes again? Are my thresholds correct?

Consider the temporal component of moments that we started with. When we don't optimally perform in the moment, it gives us an opportunity to address what got in the way and fix it. What feedback do I need? How will I be different in the next moment? When we perform well in the moment, we can build on that to be even more prepared for the next moment. Given the opportunity for a mulligan (redo), one can adjust the response for improved consequences. The exception would be busting through a threshold that has unforgiving consequences, and irreparable damage. Examples would be blowing through a threshold for drinking alcohol and receiving a DUI or chasing your attraction to someone other than your spouse and having an affair. In these cases, irreparable damage has been done and you can't take the moment back. You can't uncross the threshold. So, the questions for you would be, "Are you examining the thresholds you have?" "How disciplined are you in adhering to your established thresholds?" "How challenged are you to go beyond your perceived thresholds?"

Think of a threshold as the starting point of an experience, event, or venture. A level or point at which something will happen, or will cease to happen. Based on life learning, beliefs, character, morals, acceptance or rejection of societal standards, ability or inability to control our innermost desires, and definition of what's right and what's wrong, we all have established thresholds. These also include thresholds for our ability, our talents and skills, our physicality, our appearance, or our time.

We also have a mechanism in place to systematically assess the significant moments we confront that bump us against our established thresholds. It is here you must decide what line you

T THRESHOLD FOR DECISIONS AND ENSUING CONSEQUENCES

set for yourself and whether it is worth breaking through. Some people do this daily and some weekly. However, all effective leaders reflect on this to some capacity. For some, staying beneath the line is normal, but occasionally the tendency to go beyond the established thresholds is allowed in order to test ourselves. Once the line is breached, however, it becomes more difficult to withdraw. A complete uncontrolled breach often means a total surrender to a totally new threshold or no threshold at all.

The thresholds we set and our choices affect our health, safety, relationships, how we spend our time, and our overall well-being. They help us determine goals and direction. Moreover, and most importantly, the decisions at this point will have ensuing consequences. Some examples:

- In the moment of being approached by someone other than my spouse at an offsite seminar, is my threshold for inappropriate behavior easily allowing me to decline, or am I going to ignore my established threshold?
- In the moment of peak anger, is my threshold for control allowing me to walk away before verbally responding or sending an ill-advised email?
- In the moment of a medical diagnosis requiring changes to my physical workout and diet, is my threshold enabling me to accept or ignore that a change is required?
- In the moment of my new diet, do I give up and resolve that I'll never be able to maintain the discipline to stay the course?
- In the moment of joining a new gym and starting regular exercise, does my poor discipline lead to inconsistencies and abandonment of intent?

Exploring the notion of thresholds further, we can also look at it in terms of what is often referred to as the decision-action gap. As it relates to our current discussion, the gap can be seen as a threshold.[23] Simply put, this gap is the difference between what we want to do and what we actually do. It can be perceived as being as small as a line in the sand or a chasm that we don't know how we will cross. We say "perceived" here because the reality is that we control that gap. We determine how big or small it is. We set the distance. In the context of goal setting, we may seek to "cross our gap" for the first time. In the moment, it may cause fear and trepidation. The goal may seem too vast and unattainable. However, when we examine the gap carefully, it may result in an adjustment to the gap, and what initially seemed far may just be a limitation based on what we had thought possible (or impossible). The important word is "thought." The limitation is based on perception and not reality, even though it can seem very real in the actual moment.

Another aspect that can help us as we look at gaps is the momentum heading toward the gap. If you have already built some momentum toward the gap, this allows you to approach the gap in a different way. For example, if you are standing at a gap, there may be some limitations that impact how much of a gap you can cross. However, if you are running toward the gap, you can utilize that moment to carry yourself further. Let's put it in physical terms. If standing still, one can typically jump somewhere between 7 to 9 feet out (a bit further if you are an elite athlete). However, if running when attempting the

---

23 For more on the decision-action gap, see https://www.usafa.edu/app/uploads/21st-Century-LoC-Final-March-2021.pdf and https://jcldusafa.org/index.php/jcld/article/view/47

jump, one can extend out much further. The same idea applies to your developmental gaps as well. If you have inertia built up in your thoughts and actions, it can allow you to see your thresholds differently. However, even if you are standing still, the good news is that you can still make progress on clearing your gap.

As the decision gap allows for adjustment, our thresholds are established by what we are willing to tolerate as acceptable. Who you want to be can be overrun by who you actually are, and what you know is right can be overruled by what you actually think and want to be right. What you want to do is canceled by what you actually do. For the thresholds we establish to keep us from violating our own standards for character, personality, treatment of others, moral determinations, personal desires, anxieties, and habits, you must decide if you will hold to them or ignore them. For thresholds placing limitations on setting goals to climb to new levels of achievement, you must decide if you are willing to change your behavior, adjust your perceived threshold, and set higher standards for yourself. To better your best.

Your ability to successfully navigate your thresholds so that you can make the "right" decisions will be based in large part on how you are willing to prepare for your moments. Preparation is the key here so that when you experience the moment, you are able to discern reality versus perception. You must also recognize that without preparation, and sometimes even with preparation, the chance of failing in the moment does not always escape us. Whether our desire is to adhere to our threshold's effect on us, be it for control and keeping ourselves within what we want to be our limits, or for setting goals and going beyond what we perceive to be our limitations, when we set our plan, we need to keep in mind what are actual roadblocks and which of them are perceived. In the moment, they may seem to be one and the same. In reality, they are much different.

Chapter 16
WHAT THRESHOLDS DO I HAVE?

"If your best isn't good enough, then you need to better your best."
—Charles Lindsay

DEVELOPING YOUR THRESHOLDS is entirely personal and only you can establish them. As we have also learned, only you can navigate your choices that determine your thresholds. When you come face to face with an established threshold, each of the previous five components of the *Tempus Model* have interacted with the others, and each has been necessary for you to now meet your threshold. Seconds have passed, perhaps minutes, but the final step in your MOMENT journey has unfolded. You have now come face to face with your threshold and it's showtime. What happens from here will have consequences. So, what will YOU do?

Your threshold for the various moments you meet is typically firmly set well before you face the minute point in time. Of course, you may face unexpected thresholds and will have to react in ways never before required, or even imagined. However, for the majority of things you will face, you have already decided what your thresholds are based on numerous factors and experiences throughout life. You have been shaped from such things as what you were taught by parents or significant others in your home environment, educational experiences you have had, early relationships you were involved with, trauma you have faced, hardships you have endured, triumphs you have enjoyed, development you have purposely engaged in, and changes you intentionally instituted. No one on this earth knows you better than you.

The key is clearly understanding you and knowing unequivocally where "here" is. Is "here" truly representative of you or is it only where you would like "here" to be? Are you perfect and confident in your ability to be in control of who you are at a level that is acceptable by anyone's standard? Not knowing where "here" is can have serious, if not grave, consequences. Moreover, if you become so comfortable and naive in your acceptance of "here" and determine there is no room for improvement or constant monitoring, you may be forever jeopardizing the potential for residency in the "there." In essence, it can stunt your development before it really gets started.

Individuals have failed in their moments, and what's interesting is that it is not difficult to find examples of corporate senior officials and military leaders at all levels who have made poor decisions resulting in epic failure and life-altering consequences. Often some failures result in turnarounds and new directions. It is here at the **T** (Threshold level) where all components of the *Tempus Model* converge, and what happens from here will have consequences.

Here's another personal example of failure having pretty good consequences that happened to one of the authors (Balskus). When my dad, Joseph Bruno, passed away, I was eight years old. At that time, my three sisters and I all received a certain amount of survivor Social Security benefits that were sent to my mother up to our 18th birthday. My mom, who by the way is still rocking along at the age of 93, sat me down when I was in high school and shared with me that that money was set aside for my college, and we figured I had until age 21 to get the most out of the funds. The pressure was on. Mom, who was widowed at 34 with the four of us, instilled in us the desire to achieve more through education. We all knew we had an opportunity looking us in the face and we needed to get busy. My sister Mary was studying speech pathology and audiology and invited me to visit her and check out her program. I agreed to meet an amazing department head, Dr. Wayne Thurman, who

WHAT THRESHOLDS DO I HAVE?

walked me through the next three and a half years of my life. "If you take 12 to 13 hours of coursework in the summer and 22 course hours of work during regular semesters and maintain a B average, you will finish a dual master's before you turn 21." I dove in and in August, prior to my birthday in October, I was walking across the stage.

"Congratulations, Joe, you are now a college graduate with two master's degrees and you are 21 years old." Sounds great, but I was shaking my head and wondering where the last four years of my life had gone. I actually enjoyed the training and became a speech and language pathologist working primarily with stroke patients who suffered from adult aphasia and established myself in local hospitals. The problem was that while everyone loved my work and I cared deeply for the patients, I was an epic failure. I loved the degree, I respected the profession, but my heart was a million miles from it. I prayed about it, I agonized over it, and ultimately knew that I could not, with even a modicum of integrity, continue in a profession I did not have a passion for. It wasn't fair to the patients and was disrespectful to the profession. Bottom line, it was not my calling and I needed out.

Failing miserably is a lonely place. When everyone around you is unable to really see or relate to your internal turmoil, you go to a dark place. You question yourself. At home watching television, an Air Force commercial drew me in. That day I was in front of the recruiter, asking to test for Officer Training School. In October, one and a half years from my graduation with my master's, I was standing outside the gate of the Air Force Officer Training School thanking God that my failure had led to change and total elation about a new career and direction! I still recall the Air Force recruiter saying, "Let me get this straight. You have two master's degrees, a great job and career, and you want to sign up for the Air Force?" I'm grateful every day that I said yes!

Life sometimes leads us in directions we don't understand. When you have gone in a direction that feels good and right at the time, you can tend to accept it and be fearful of change. You may feel you are disappointing others. Others may disappoint you and fail to understand the decisions you are making. Pushing through the perceived failure and establishing new thresholds is something that you can greatly benefit from. This can apply to something as complex as a career change, or as simple as an exercise goal. Here is a quote I came up with that has helped me in my journey:

> *"It's never too late to do the things today that you thought were gone yesterday."* —Joseph Balskus

Place into your head an imaginary line that hovers over your mind and your heart at all times. Many things may take you right up to the line, while others may cause you to hang out just below the line and occasionally try to peek beyond the line. Some may cause you to run parallel with the line while you decide whether to retreat or disregard. How solid are the established thresholds you have? Are they real or are they only perceived and flexible? If real, do you have the capacity to stop at the line or perhaps run parallel to the line, or is your threshold line perceived and flexible, offering you an opportunity to continue as if it didn't even exist? The perceived line can be stopping you from advancing toward a

WHAT THRESHOLDS DO I HAVE?

place you want to be as in the case of a run time or a weight loss goal. It can also be a line that you want to adhere to but given the right circumstance, you could easily adjust and completely change direction. In all cases, whether confronting a real or perceived threshold, you will need to decide to accept, reject, or adjust what you do next. From this, you either continue forward or retreat, and from here on there will be ensuing consequences.

This imaginary line is what we call the *Threshold Tolerance Line* (TTL) (Figure B).

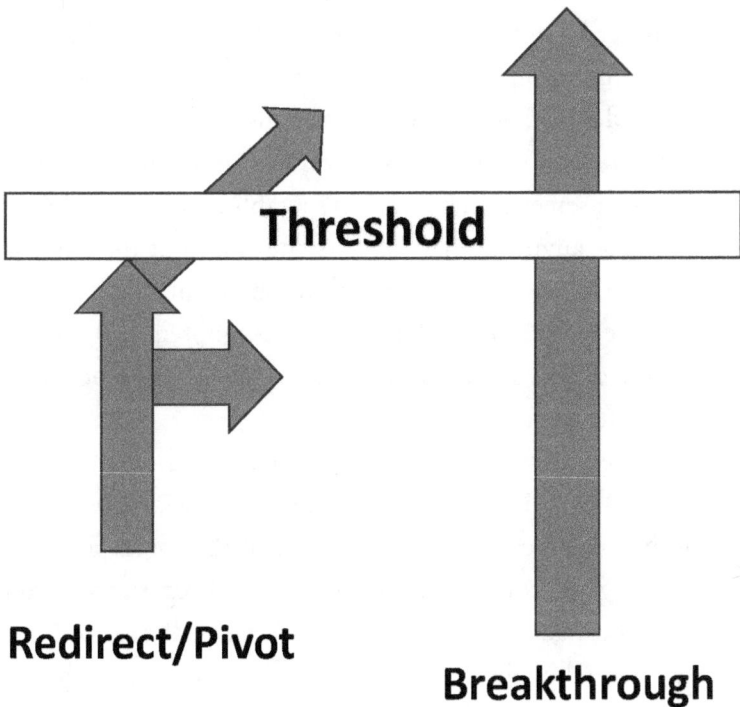

Figure B: Threshold Tolerance Line (TTL)

For example, based on experience, family or professional responsibility, or what you've determined to be responsible behavior, you have established a threshold for drinking. In the moment of reacting to a stressful day and having a desire to forget the reason for the stress, you stop off to have a drink at your favorite local establishment. Coming up on your threshold that you know is your limit, you are reminded of the stress that brought you here. When confronting the line, you reject it and make a decision. You deserve another drink and need to forget. So, you forge ahead and continue to drink. A decision was made about a threshold and a consequence will ensue.

Another would be the student faced with a deadline and with no time to prepare for an upcoming test. The student is approached by someone who possesses answers to the questions likely to be asked by the same professor who taught the course the previous semester. The student's established threshold is to never accept anything that suggests cheating, but the stress is overwhelming and the established threshold, in the moment, is overcome by emotion. The threshold is ignored, and the answers are accepted and used. Again, there are consequences that will ensue from the broken threshold.

Perceived thresholds are those that may hold us back from who we really want to be, which can work for or against us. If you have a perceived rather than a real threshold, you will relax during the confrontation and totally disregard what you thought you had set as a threshold. We have all read of cases where those thought to have impeccable character behaved in such ways as to warrant dismissal from high positions of leadership. We have been shocked to read of those who exhibited poor and damaging moral behavior, those who have been

WHAT THRESHOLDS DO I HAVE?

removed for caustic leadership practices, and those who seemingly were one way on the outside, but someone totally and despicably ugly on the inside.

We have witnessed CEO's being removed for unethical practices, general officers demoted and disgraced for inappropriate behavior, cadets dismissed for honor code violations, political figures disgraced for misappropriation of funds and money laundering. It is the total disregard for what most would agree should be thresholds in exchange for flexibility based on what you're really made of on the inside. It applies to those who wish to hide behind a public exterior and camouflage an interior they hope no one will ever see.

Conversely, if you have a perceived threshold that limits your ability to accomplish beyond a certain level of performance, you will need to evaluate this and adjust or recalibrate a new, much higher, and improved threshold. As an example, for one working on a PhD, it is well publicized that many start and few finish. Only 1 percent of the world's 25- to 64-year-olds who have been to university have a PhD, but over double that actually begin the process. In an article published by *The Chronicle of Higher Education* entitled "How Much Is Too Much?,"[24] the current PhD attrition rate is approximately 50%.

Research indicates most PhD applicants have never experienced a journey quite like it before, so they have nothing to which they can compare it. Expectations and abstract concepts sometimes don't match reality, so as students matriculate, they finally experience what they had up until now only been imagining. Coming face to face with this, they may decide it's not

---

24 https://www.chronicle.com/article/ph-d-attrition-how-much-is-too-much/

for them. Those who complete the journey, on the other hand, face the perceived and imagined experience by adjusting and reevaluating how much they want it and whether the sacrifice is worth the journey. New expectations are set, goals are reestablished and redirected, and deep breaths are taken to overcome the obstacles in order to complete the challenge.

When faced with real or perceived thresholds, one might say it comes down to the heart and once again, how you want to show up. Only you can determine your *threshold tolerance line*. It is the intrinsic motivation and the intentional pursuit that will determine your fate. Can you pause long enough to consider the consequences of your actions? Can you overcome the influences of your past to determine the correct choices? Will you adhere to or blow through the thresholds that are embedded into who you are? Do you have the strength and courage to accept that you are "here," and that if you are ever going to be "there," adjustments need to be made and made NOW!

What thresholds do you have? If you adhere to or break through thresholds in your personal life, do they have an effect on how you address those in your professional life? Only you know. And what of the other side of your thresholds? We have discussed how breaking through or ignoring thresholds can impact the next steps in where you are going and fuel the iteration of you that you allow to proceed. That you ultimately want to proceed. If you successfully hide who you are and fool everyone around you, are you willing to take the gamble that this will last forever or for as long as you need it to? Will you continue to hide in the moments, or will you be found out?

How will you react when confronting face to face the reality of your real or perceived thresholds? Only you can decide.

WHAT THRESHOLDS DO I HAVE?

Bruno had little Joe gaze into the mirror for a reason. "Smile. Okay, you look pretty good. In fact, it's likely you will be the most handsome boy in church today." But as the finger came over the shoulder and he confronted his son with the reality of the heart, the real question came out: "How are you doing, in 'here'?" Yes, your moments are determined by your established thresholds, but the consequences are more profoundly determined by your acceptance, rejection, or adjustment of the threshold you are encountering. Do you retreat? Break through? Redirect? Is the line a barrier to your growth? What's on the other side? Is it worth it?

We would like to offer some questions for you to thoughtfully consider as you think about your "Thresholds for decisions and ensuing consequences."

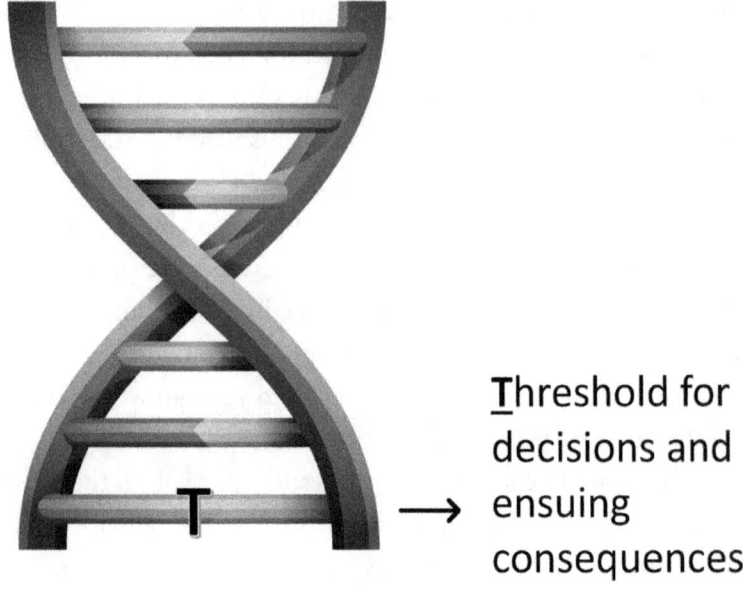

Threshold for decisions and ensuing consequences

**Reflection Questions for "T":
Threshold for decisions and ensuing consequences**

Take a few minutes to reflect on the following questions:

1.) Do I know my established thresholds for various areas of my life?
    - What are some of them?
        - Are they real?
        - Are they perceived?

2.) When it comes to maintaining high standards in terms of what I believe to be right/wrong, good/bad, moral/immoral, am I pleased with my thresholds or do I need to make any adjustments?

WHAT THRESHOLDS DO I HAVE?

3.) When it comes to setting goals, have I created gaps between what I want to do and what I actually do?

4.) What adjustments do I feel are necessary in understanding and living by my thresholds?

5.) What adjustments do I feel are necessary to close the gaps in my perceived limitations to set and commit to my goals?

Chapter 17

HOW CAN I BE SURE?

THE POWER OF ACCOUNTABILITY

"It's not only what we do, but also what we do not do, for which we are accountable."
—Molière

THE OPPORTUNITY HERE is that we can create an architecture of support around this entire process of development in and for the MOMENT. The primary way to do that is to develop an accountability structure that informs and aids us in our development. Some questions we will naturally have are:

- How do we know how we are showing up?
- How do we know if we are making progress?
- How do we know if we are closing the gap(s) between where I am and where I want to be?
- What goals have I accomplished?
- Do my goals need to change?

If we are going to be intentional about our development and maximize the moments in our lives, then we need to make sure that we stay on the track that we set for ourselves. That statement bears repeating. We need to make sure that we stay on the track that WE set for ourselves. This is our journey ... our developmental trajectory. We set the stage. How can we ensure that we are showing up to the moments the right way to be able to break through our thresholds?

The good news is that there are numerous ways to do this. The key is to find the one that works for you. There is no single size that fits all. Just as there is no one size that fits all in leadership development regardless of what some may want you to think. But, there is one size that fits YOU and YOUR development. During executive coaching, it is common for the coachee to ask, "What do I need to do?" A seasoned coach doesn't take the bait and provide the answer because they know that unless the coachee is committed to the process (the work) and struggles a bit with the hard truth, it is unlikely to be successful. Instead, the coach will guide the coachee through a process of self-discovery where the coachee develops a plan that they are committed to. That is fundamental to intentional leadership development. It is not something that is provided to us. It is something that we have to seek and experience. Otherwise, it won't last. Coaching can be a very successful way to work on your leader development, as it has been shown to be linked to such outcomes as improved work performance, increased team effectiveness, greater self-confidence, more effective communication skills, improved wellness, and better work-life balance.

A mentor can also be helpful in this process, as they provide a different perspective than a coach. In many cases the mentor has been through what you have been through. They can provide contextual considerations as well as guide points to help you on your way. When paired with a coach, you can get a holistic perspective of where you want to go, what you can expect along the way, and how you can be successful.

While not everyone has an executive coach to work with, you aren't starting from scratch. You know you. Or at least you think you do. What you need to do is to have a process in place so that you can objectively determine how you are doing. You don't want to go through all of the processes of understanding where "here" is and where "there" needs to be and then not know how you are doing or if you are even making progress.

This brings up a critical component of accountability, which is assessment. As part of your plan, you must be diligent in getting the information you need. Not the information you want, or just using the information that is readily available to you. If you are going to lean in and maximize your moments, shouldn't you at least be just as focused on finding out if you are making progress. If you are not progressing in an area, you need to know that just like you need to know if you are progressing in an area.

A common way to get this assessment is through 360-degree feedback, as we have talked about previously. This type of feedback is particularly useful because of the richness of data it can provide. 360-degree feedback is called that because it provides information at various points around you. This is particularly robust feedback because you can get an idea of how you are showing up with different constituencies that you come into contact with. This allows us to see where there might be deficiencies so that we can target our development. If the questions are aligned specifically with our developmental plan, it is possible to see how we are doing at various levels with the specific parts of our plan.

One key aspect with respect to 360-degree feedback is that you must be very aware of who you are soliciting feedback from. If you only choose those who will be "nice" or supportive in their ratings, then you limit your ability to get honest and constructive feedback. If you don't have an accurate picture, it can halt or stunt your development. So, as part of the 360-degree feedback process (and really any feedback process you use to support your development), you must think through questions such as:

- Who are you currently getting feedback from?
- Who do you need to hear from?
- Who has good visibility of your behavior and can give you detailed feedback?

- Who is in a position to assess your development?
- Who do you need to get feedback from that you may not want to?
- Who can I share my feedback with to help hold me accountable to my developmental goals?

The more honest and truthful you are, the more likely that you will get feedback that will help you developmentally, which will help you to prepare for your moments.

While formal assessment methodologies can provide detailed information to you, data collection methods don't always have to be so sophisticated. It could be as simple as someone observing your behavior from time to time and letting you know when there is an inconsistency. You could also set up a feedback process where you get feedback from others periodically on how you are doing. This doesn't have to be an arduous formal undertaking. It does, however, need to be consistent. Finally, you can also incorporate a habit of reflection where you can reexamine situations (positive and negative) and think about your actions and if they moved you closer to or further away from your intended purpose. This not only helps you to lead and act consistently, but also to prepare to engage in the moments when they arise and deal with your thresholds.

While we have been speaking largely about accountability and assessment geared toward our specific goals, the reality is that sometimes things need to change (think back to the different types of moments we brought up in chapter 4). As a result of our moments, sometimes we need to pivot. We may need a different direction. We need to ask ourselves, "Do we have a process in place to reevaluate and modify our goals, if necessary?" Things change and we may need to as well. In the military, we use the saying coined by Field Marshal Helmuth von Moltke that *"No plan survives contact with the enemy."* That happens in our lives as well. It can be by choices we make, sometimes by factors outside our control, or it can be from a threshold that is breached. From a planning and accountability standpoint, we want to make sure we have a plan in place (even if we need to modify it) so that we can account for and maneuver within the moments we encounter.

As we have mentioned several times in this book so far, reflection is a critical component of leadership development. As a guide to support you in your development, we offer two checklists at the end of this chapter. The first one is focused as you are coming up to a significant moment. It is a tool to help you make sure that you are prepared for the moment. The second is designed to be used after the moment (during reflection) to see how you did. Did you show up the way that you intended? Did you break through a threshold? This reflection process can be incredibly useful not just after expected moments, but especially when you reflect back on those moments that were unexpected and uncontrolled.

We say we offer these because their real value is not in stepping through them exactly every single time in a rote manner. Instead, they are offered as a way to help develop processes to think through the needed aspects of a moment ahead of time. And, again, as a way of reflecting on the moment after it has passed to review "how you did" with respect to how you wanted to do.

Tempus Checklist (Pre-Moment)

	Component	Questions to Consider
M	Minute points in time that present	• Why is this moment significant? • Is this a new type of moment? • How do my past experiences impact how I am showing up to this moment?
O	Opportunities that	• What opportunities are present in the upcoming moment? • How am I perceiving the opportunities? • How am I approaching this moment (+/-)? • What does "success" look like for this moment?
M	Manifest into actions	• What actions are possible? • Are there any actions to be avoided? • What actions am I willing to take in this moment? • What do I need to do to prepare for this moment?

THE POWER OF ACCOUNTABILITY

E	Empowering us to	• Am I in a position of influence? • Do I have control over the situation? • Do I feel like I can be successful in this moment? • Is there a barrier I need to be aware of (internal or external)?
N	Navigate choices which determine our	• Where am I as I am heading into the moment? • Where do I want to be after this moment? • What options are available to me in this moment? • Where is "here" for me in this moment? • What choice do I need to make in this moment?
T	Threshold for decisions and ensuing consequences	• Is there a threshold for this moment that I need to be aware of (perceived or actual)? • If yes, what is stopping me from moving past the threshold? • What are the likely consequences of this moment based on my actions?

Tempus Checklist (Post-Moment)

	Component	Reflection Questions
T	Thresholds in my life were faced successfully by	• Was there a threshold for this moment that I should have been aware of (perceived or actual)? • If yes, why was I not aware of it? • What are the consequences of the moment based on my actions? • Did I cross a threshold in the moment? • What does that mean for me going forward?
N	Navigating my choices which	• Where was I as I was heading into the moment? • What were my choices/options in the moment? • What is my new "here" after the moment?
E	Empowered me through the	• Was I in a position of influence in the moment? • Did I have control over the situation? • Was there a barrier I needed to be aware of (internal or external)? • Did I feel prepared for the moment?

M	Manifested actions I chose during my	• What actions were possible in the moment? • What actions did I take in the moment? • Were there any actions to be avoided? Did I? • Was I successful in the moment?
O	Opportunities in the	• What opportunities were present in the upcoming moment? • How did I perceive the opportunities? • Did my approach (+/-) impact the moment? • Did I understand all of the opportunities that were available to me in the moment?
M	Minute points in time that I encountered	• Why was the moment significant? • Was this a new type of moment? • How did my past experiences impact how I showed up to the moment? • How will this moment impact my future moments?

Chapter 18
WHAT THIS MEANS FOR YOU

"You can't prepare for every moment, but you can prepare YOU for every moment."
—Douglas Lindsay

IN OUR OPENING story, Bruno had an opportunity in his short life to react to and lean into his moments. Using that as an entry point, we worked through the *Tempus Model*. We hope this model will be a steady source of understanding and reflection for you.

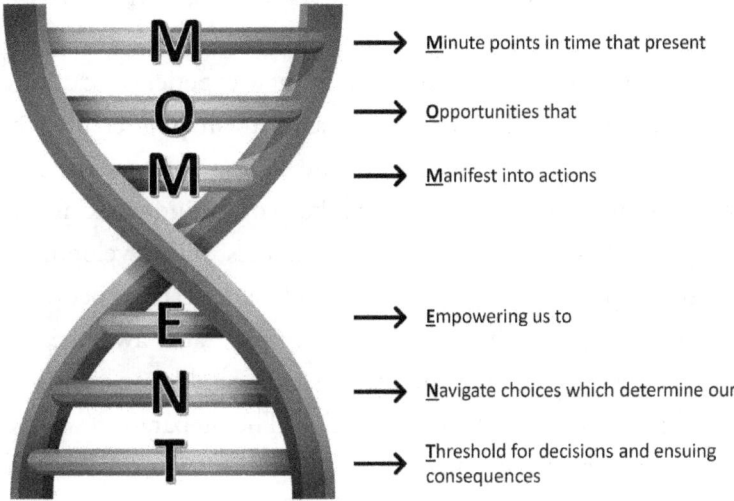

→ **M**inute points in time that present

→ **O**pportunities that

→ **M**anifest into actions

→ **E**mpowering us to

→ **N**avigate choices which determine our

→ **T**hreshold for decisions and ensuing consequences

The question for you is, how will you prepare yourself for your moments? We are all unique creatures who have developed based on a number of factors, some of which are upbringing, family, friends, teachers, coaches, educational experiences, beliefs, and religion/faith. We need to work to understand our past experiences and embedded tendencies to understand how they impact what we do now, in our present moments. Understanding ourselves and how we were shaped by these past experiences assists with the analysis of our inner, intrinsic nature. This helps us make conscious, intentional decisions to train in qualities that strengthen awareness and motivation to develop. Understanding ourselves and our past experiences helps us analyze our drive and discipline to push beyond our self-imposed limitations and thresholds. These thresholds need to be constantly evaluated to see if adjustment is needed. This involves a daily walk and conscious effort to train ourselves to a higher standard, and this training must be consistent.

Just as past experiences shape us, new experiences can help change our perception of life and assist in shaping us into the person we want to become. If we are willing to invest the time and energy into learning, this will keep our mind working and keep us on a trajectory toward awareness and development. Preparing for the moments in your life is a steady process, involving diligence, discipline, and an immutable awareness of your inner, intrinsic thresholds. These thresholds can vary from strong to seemingly weak and flexible. The preparation we take to understand these thresholds determines the outcome and consequence.

We have mentioned throughout this book the need to be prepared for the moments you face. Preparation requires action and intentionality on your part. This is not an easy task as research has shown one's concentration is affected by such everyday things as worries, irrelevant thoughts, and distractions from events or emotions.[25] In addition, our productivity is affected by attentional control and our ability to focus on a task.[26]

---

25 Tyng, C., Amin, H., Saad, M., & Malik, A. (2017). The influences of emotion on learning and memory. *Frontiers in Psychology*, 1454.
26 Langner, R., & Eickhoff, S. (2013). Sustaining attention to simple tasks: A meta-analytic review of the neural mechanisms of vigilant attention. *Psychological Bulletin, 139(4)*, 870.

WHAT THIS MEANS FOR YOU

These present developmental challenges to us as leaders, and we must focus on numerous aspects throughout multiple divisions of the organization while being responsible for the success of operations and the leadership of the people in the organization. Moreover, leaders have a personal responsibility to the members of the organization to exercise mental clarity and maintain emotional readiness to perform. If you lose your focus, mental clarity, and emotional intelligence, the outcome and consequence of your moment will be much different. If you can maintain focus in your moments, the goal you thought to be unattainable becomes predictably more achievable.

Ultimately, it comes down to YOU. You individually have been shaped by your past and you have opportunities each day to be strengthened by new experiences, new challenges, fresh learning opportunities, renewed relationships and friendships, and challenging goals for improvement. You can strive to be the person who reflects outwardly what you feel and want to be inwardly, because you are able to stand up proudly at every threshold you meet and proudly receive the reward of the consequence of the moment. We can see this as we walk our moment back:

IN YOUR MOMENT

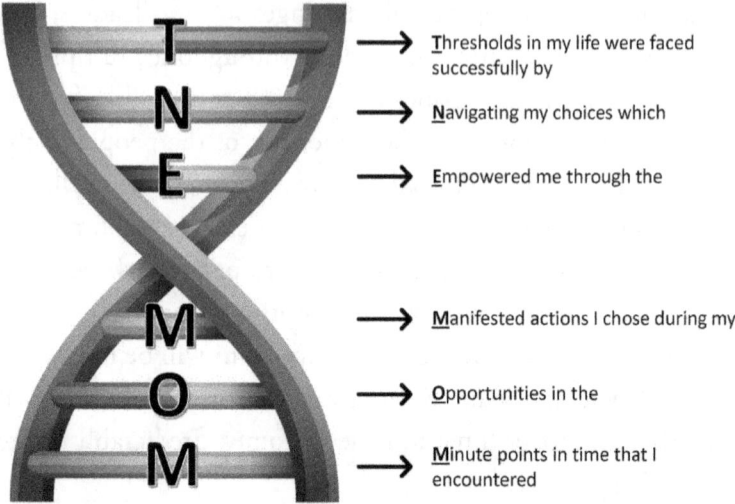

→ **T**hresholds in my life were faced successfully by

→ **N**avigating my choices which

→ **E**mpowered me through the

→ **M**anifested actions I chose during my

→ **O**pportunities in the

→ **M**inute points in time that I encountered

What you want to be able to say is that the consequences have been incredibly rewarding and fulfilling, that you have bettered yourself, your family, and those you lead. You want to be able to reflect on life and see that your preparedness, your commitment and decisiveness, helped you pull back from a bad decision in the moment. You want to see the benefit of pushing beyond a perceived threshold, resulting in a better you … more physically fit, more financially secure, more spiritually fulfilled. We all want to succeed and have lives we can be proud of. Ultimately, we want to have a greater and more meaningful life experience that makes us and all those around us better.

As we think about moving forward, let's remember the poignant words of Mahatma Gandhi: *"The future depends on what you do today."* We would like to add to that by stating that *"Your development depends on how you maximize your moments today."*

Chapter 19
YOUR TURN

"Tell me and I forget. Teach me and I remember. Involve me and I learn."
—Benjamin Franklin

WHAT WILL BE your next moment when your continuum unfolds? How will your opportunities manifest into actions? Will you prepare and empower yourself to navigate your choices? Will your decisions adhere to or challenge your established thresholds? What consequences do you want to achieve? We would posit for consideration, it is time for contemplation about your preparedness and training. It is important to have a conscious awareness of the inevitability of your moments, and it is critical to recognize the power of those moments and the potential impact they afford. Moments have consequences. If your moments are met with weakness or confusion, or navigated with uncertainty and unbridled, careless, and unconstrained choices, the consequences could be calamitous. If your moments are approached with preparedness, and if navigated with certainty as you come face to face with what you believe to be thresholds, the consequences could be advantageous, even providential.

Leaders who experience the most success have learned to maintain a set of standards that include a balanced combination of ethics, morals, behaviors, and discipline. This equilibrium has enabled them to consistently make the right decisions and successfully navigate their choices. Yet, even the most successful leaders inevitably face the occasional struggles that lurk inside each of us and can potentially draw us toward inappropriate reactions, immoral choices, unethical behavior, or just bad decisions that have negative consequences. This can happen when leaders lose sight of who they are as a leader. What we mean is that core set of beliefs (or standards) that define them as a leader.

Our moments have an enduring impact on how we are

showing up as a leader. Do those moments move us closer to who we say we are as a leader or do they move us further away? Regardless of what we choose, they necessarily have an impact on our development. If we accept the notion of *"who you are is how you lead,"* as proposed by Robert Hogan and Robert Kaiser,[27] then our leadership behaviors are a manifestation of the choices we make in our moments.

Throughout this book, we brought things to the forefront for contemplation and offered some moments you can prepare for and others that offer no such luxury. Some are completely unexpected. The question you (as we all) must address is, "What are you going to do to prepare yourself for such a time when you are 'In Your Moment'?" In addition, what will you take away and apply from the information that was presented so that you can prepare for your next moment?

Our hope is that through the process of reading this book, you were able to increase your awareness of the concept of being "In Your Moment." Don't forget, moments are important and represent increments of learning and development. You will frame the moments or the moments will frame you. You should draw strength and encouragement from the *Tempus Model* depicting key words and phrases within the MOMENT. We offer it as a model that compels you to venture inside its core and verify its applicability in your life. Use it and refer back to it for a reminder of the significance of each letter of M O M E N T.

Thank you for joining us on this journey. For now, we

---

[27] Hogan, R., & Kaiser, R. (2005). What we know about leadership. *Review of General Psychology, 9(2)*, No. 2, 169–180.

encourage you to close this book slowly and think about where you are. Consider:

- Where is your "here"?
- Are you where you want to be?
- What moment are you facing?
- What moment will be unexpectedly thrust upon you?
- What moment are you considering?
- Are you prepared?
- What are you willing to commit to your moment?
- Are you examining your thresholds?
- Are you willing to accept the consequences?

"As a man thinks
in his heart, so is he."
—Proverbs 23:7(a)

About the Authors

Dr. Douglas R. Lindsay

Dr. Lindsay began his career by attending the United States Air Force Academy, where he graduated with Military Distinction and received a commission in the U.S. Air Force. He served for over 22 years in a multitude of roles, including research psychologist, occupational analyst, inspector general, deputy squadron commander, senior military professor, full professor, deputy department head, and research center director, in addition to a deployment to Afghanistan supporting Operation ENDURING FREEDOM. Since leaving the military, he has worked for numerous higher education institutions, businesses, and consulting organizations developing leadership programs and educational courses focused on executive education and development at multiple Fortune 100 companies. This included a role as a professor and the founding director of the Master of Professional Studies Program in the Psychology of Leadership at Pennsylvania State University. In addition to his consulting and coaching, he is the founder and Executive Editor for the *Journal of Character & Leadership Development* (www.jcldusafa.org) at the United States Air Force Academy.

Dr. Lindsay is widely published with over 150 articles, chapters, and books on leadership and leadership development. He is a sought-after speaker, facilitator, author, and executive coach, helping organizations develop evidence-based leadership programs to facilitate leader and character development.

He received a Bachelor's degree in Behavioral Sciences from the United States Air Force Academy, a Master's degree in Experimental Psychology from the University of Texas at San Antonio, and a PhD in Industrial/Organizational Psychology concentrating on leadership from The Pennsylvania State University. He has been married to his wife, Karina, for over 31 years and has a daughter, Mariah, and two sons, Malek and Cole.

Dr. Joseph G. Balskus

Dr. Balskus accepted a commission in the United States Air Force, graduating from Officer Training School on February 14, 1980, as a Distinguished Graduate. His career spanned over 35 years, serving on Air Force Active duty, the Air Force Reserve, and Air National Guard. He was selected and confirmed by the U.S. Senate to the rank of Brigadier General in 2002, and for over seven years served as the Assistant Adjutant General for Air and commander of the Florida Air National Guard. After serving as the National Chairman of the Air National Guard Strategic Planning System, he was nominated and confirmed by the Senate to Major General and assigned as the Military Assistant to the Deputy Chief of Staff, Strategic Plans and Requirements, at the Pentagon. He became the Air Force architect for the establishment of the Total Force Task Force and testified before Congress during the 2014 National Commission on the Structure of the Air Force.

Dr. Balskus is an accomplished writer, a sought-after speaker, and an organizational leader with extensive background

ABOUT THE AUTHORS

and experience in leadership, motivational education, and executive coaching. He obtained his PhD from Grand Canyon University in psychology with an emphasis on performance psychology, and has published his extensive research on the relationship of spiritual intelligence and moral potency in United States military leaders.

He is the recipient of numerous awards and decorations, including the Air Force Distinguished Service Medal and two awards of the state of Florida's highest award, The Florida Cross. He has extensive senior executive education, including Harvard JFK School of Government and Syracuse University Defense Studies, and he has been included in the Eastern Illinois University Outstanding Alumni group and the Westville Illinois High School Wall of Honor. He has been married to the former Lisa Brooker for the past 40 years, and they have a son, Brandon, and two daughters, Brittany and Courtney.

Moving Forward:

Dr. Lindsay and Dr. Balskus have spent decades teaching, coaching, speaking, and delivering workshops on all aspects of leadership including the topics discussed in this book.

If you are interested in working with them or would like more information, please reach out to them at: www.InYourMoment.org